94. Russell Eveh

Caroline Elizabe...

Dave Goss

Thank you for all you do,
Jonathan Campbell

Bill Downing

Hank Jenkins

Paul Crikelair
Philippians 1:3-6
George Simpson

Joel Day

Lisa & John McKee

Greg Edwards

Ben Bush

Bev Hall

Randy Williams

Jeanne Maddox III

Ruthann Simpson

Esther Choi

Thank you for your intentional invitation to NCC!
Jennifer Ann Smith

Disability, Faith, and the Church

Disability, Faith, and the Church

Inclusion and Accommodation in Contemporary Congregations

Courtney Wilder

PRAEGER™

An Imprint of ABC-CLIO, LLC
Santa Barbara, California • Denver, Colorado

Library of Congress Cataloging-in-Publication Data

Names: Wilder, Courtney, author.
Title: Disability, faith, and the church : inclusion and accommodation in contemporary
    congregations / Courtney Wilder.
Description: Santa Barbara : Praeger, 2016. | Includes bibliographical references and index.
Identifiers: LCCN 2015051195 | ISBN 9781440838842 (hardcopy : alk. paper) |
    ISBN 9781440838859 (ebook)
Subjects: LCSH: Church work with people with disabilities. | Disabilities—Religious
    aspects—Christianity.
Classification: LCC BV4460 .W475 2016 | DDC 261.8/324—dc23
LC record available at http://lccn.loc.gov/2015051195

ISBN: 978–1–4408–3884–2
EISBN: 978–1–4408–3885–9

20 19 18 17 16   1 2 3 4 5

This book is also available on the World Wide Web as an eBook.
Visit www.abc-clio.com for details.

Praeger
An Imprint of ABC-CLIO, LLC

ABC-CLIO, LLC
130 Cremona Drive, P.O. Box 1911
Santa Barbara, California 93116-1911

This book is printed on acid-free paper ∞

Manufactured in the United States of America

To Grace and Peter Klinefelter, whose unflagging enthusiasm
for all things is a joy to behold

Contents

Acknowledgments

I owe tremendous thanks to the many people who provided support, encouragement, and feedback during the writing of this book. The leaders of ministries profiled in the book were gracious with their time, welcoming as I got to know their communities, and patient with my many questions: thanks to Debbie Buchholz, Mary Ann Kelly-Wright, Carol Tillman, and their respective congregations, Deaf International Community Church, St. Joan of Arc's, and Rejoice! Lutheran Church. Equally generous were the religious leaders who agreed to be interviewed: thanks to Craig Satterlee, Kirk VanGilder, Erin Diericx, and Raedorah Stewart. Any mistakes in describing these congregations or leaders are my own.

Many other friends and colleagues provided thoughtful feedback as I wrote the book. Friends in the Association of Teaching Theologians offered insights that I returned to again and again. ELCA staff including Ron Duty and Mark Wilhelm provided me with important documents and responded at length to my many questions. Jeremy Rehwaldt and Donna Lanclos were great first readers whose feedback helped shape my argument in many places. Debbie Creamer was both encouraging and thoughtful in her responses to my inquiries. Many of my students asked questions or made observations about disability and faith that pointed me in new and interesting directions, and the support from students and colleagues at Midland University is much appreciated.

Chapter 3 is based on a paper entitled "Luther, Swinton, and the Vanishing Self: Christ's Power over Despair, Suicide and Dementia" presented at the American Academy of Religion Meeting, Martin Luther and Global Studies section, in November 2014. Many thanks to Ted Peters for his appreciative response to that paper and to Vitor Westhelle for his thoughtful comments.

Chapter 4 includes work that was originally published as a column in *Sightings*, an online publication of the Martin Marty Center at the University of Chicago Divinity School, called "Valuing All Human Beings: Disability and Reproductive Rights Meet Congress," in January 2013, and other work originally presented in a conference paper at the Upper Midwest American Academy of Religion Meeting in April 2013, entitled "Feminism, Reproductive Rights, and Disability: Conflicting Accounts of Autonomy." My UMAAR colleagues have created an energetic and supportive intellectual community for students and faculty alike.

Finally, the support of the members of my congregation, Augustana Lutheran in Omaha, Nebraska, is invaluable to me. Both as I wrote and as I recovered from surgery that was scheduled midway through the writing process, my community offered encouragement, asked great questions, provided feedback, and cared for me and my children. Participation in the life of my congregation continues to renew my belief in the value of community as a religious force.

CHAPTER ONE

Introduction to Disability Theology

Introduction

Recently, at a conference I met a young man who is a seminary student. Over lunch, he talked about how he discerned a call for ministry. When he was a child, his parents had left the church, but his grandmother had helped him become familiar with stories from the Bible, and as a high school and college student he was increasingly drawn to religion and ultimately to a calling to ministry. Curious, I asked what caused his parents to leave their church. He said it wasn't only one congregation that they had left, but Christianity as a whole. He explained that as a child, his sister had an expressive speech disorder. Other people, including other children, often did not understand her speech. When they were together, he could help translate for her and provided a social buffer for her. However, in Sunday School, they were consistently separated. Without his presence and protection, she was routinely ridiculed by other kids. In none of the congregations the family attended was the Sunday School prepared to create an environment where she was welcomed and not subject to teasing and rejection from other children. They tried several churches, and in each place, the story was the same. Ultimately, his parents decided that if this was Christianity, it wasn't for them. There was no place for their child, and thus no place for them, to be recognized as part of the family of the church.

The story ends well for this young man and his sister in terms of their reconciliation to Christianity; they are now adults both involved in Christian congregations. However, their parents have not rejoined a church and took some time to accept their son's call to ministry. What might have seemed like a minor distraction or an unimportant discipline problem to a series of Sunday School teachers led to a fracture between this family and Christianity. The parents could not reconcile the treatment their daughter experienced with the promises and expectations of shared Christian life. Perhaps, the teachers did all they could; perhaps, they did not have the resources to create classrooms where each child was comfortable and safe and able to learn the gospel. They may not have had any experience with children with speech disorders; likely they were not trained professionals, but volunteers. Regardless of the reasons, the impact on this family was significant.

This is not, unfortunately, an unusual story. As we will see, people with disabilities have routinely experienced what theologian Thomas Reynolds calls "theologically denigrating views of disability [that] diminish the creaturely worth of persons with disability, overlooking the broader vision of inclusive love and hospitality to which the biblical text bears witness."[1] People living with disabilities are regularly excluded from Christian communities and positions of leadership in those communities. Christian scripture may or may not be interpreted as liberating to people with disabilities, and preaching and worship services may reinforce rather than reject biases against people with disabilities. This book explores disability as a bodily, cultural, and religious phenomenon, and I argue that while Christian churches and people have regularly failed to recognize the value and the gifts of people with disabilities both in teaching and in practice, in the biblical tradition and in Christian life, people with disabilities are present, faithful, and responding to the call to lead.

What Is Disability?

One central question we need to consider is: What is disability? In one sense, as a feature of human embodiment, disability has been a part of our shared experience forever. In another sense, the idea of disability as a political and social and religious category is relatively new. Various models of understanding disability, some more constructive than others, have influenced theological constructs of disability and religious practices. To begin with, language to describe disability is somewhat contested. While the term "disability" is standard among scholars and theologians of disability, and "people with disabilities" is a phrase I will use throughout this book, there are other terms. Some people prefer "differently abled"; others use the shorthand "special needs." Disability rights activists, including for example Harriet McBryde Johnson, whose work we will consider in Chapter 4, sometimes use the term "crip." On the other hand, many Deaf people do not regard themselves as disabled and describe Deaf people as a cultural minority. I have defaulted to what is known as "people first" language—*person with an intellectual disability, person living with a disability*, and so on—but I recommend that the individual preferences of people with disabilities be honored in the context of congregational life.

The Social Model

What are the prevailing constructs of disability? Lennard Davis, an expert in disability studies, describes the social model of disability, which distinguishes between cultural and bodily experience:

> Contemporary theoreticians of disability distinguish between an impairment and a disability. An impairment is a physical fact, but a disability is a social construction. For example, lack of mobility is an impairment, but an environment without ramps turns that impairment into a disability. ... I define physical disability as a disruption in the sensory field of the observer. ... The term disability is tied to the development of discourses that aim to cure, remediate, or catalog variations in bodies.[2]

This claim, that disability is socially constructed, means that the location of disability is not in the body of the person who is impaired, but in the social response to that person: a person using a wheelchair moves along just fine, for example, until she encounters a set of stairs without a ramp or an elevator nearby. Many disability rights activists and theologians of disability affirm this model and resist what is called the medical model of disability, and the related rehabilitation model.

The Medical and Rehabilitation Models

The medical model of disability tends to focus on what the individual body cannot do, often with the goal of intervening and treating the person so that his or her body is, or seems, more in keeping with the "normal" body. Unlike the social model, the medical and rehabilitation models identify disability as a problem within the body of the person living with disability. Davis writes, "The medical model treats disability as a disease in need of a cure, while the rehabilitation model sees it as a body in need of repair, concealment, remediation, and supervision."[3] The medical model would explain the problem of a person in a wheelchair encountering stairs with no ramp or elevator nearby as a problem with her bodily mobility, not with the building's lack of accessibility. The rehabilitation model might suggest medical intervention in the form of a prosthetic limb, rather than a ramp, as the solution to her problem of access. Of course, people with and without disabilities benefit from medical care. However, if the medical and rehabilitation models are the primary means of understanding the body, it can be construed as defective. Rejecting this construct of disability allows for the positive and affirming understanding of their own bodies that many people with disabilities experience. This shifts the obligation for access from the body (and the individual) to the social structure. It also opens the way for critique of social and religious norms as the locus of problems for people with disabilities.

The Minority Group Model

Davis describes a third model of understanding disability, the minority group model: he points out that people with disabilities "make up 12 to 15 percent of the population—a greater proportion than any other minority."[4] Like other minority groups, people with disabilities experience discrimination and a shared identity as "other," over and against a more socially powerful normative group. Focusing on a shared cultural experience is particularly resonant among Deaf and DeafBlind people, many of whom identify strongly as participants in a cultural minority rather than as people with disabilities. Davis writes, "[M]any Deaf activists do not consider themselves disabled. Rather, the Deaf think of themselves as a linguistic minority like Latinos or Asians, who are defined by their use of a language other than the dominant one in the United States."[5] As we will see, Deaf churches reflect this cultural norm.[6]

The recognition of people with disabilities as a minority social group is codified in the Americans with Disabilities Act (ADA), which reads in part:

> To be protected by the ADA, one must have a disability, which is defined by the ADA as a physical or mental impairment that substantially limits one or more major life activities, a person who has a history or record of such an impairment, or a person who is perceived by others as having such an impairment. The ADA does not specifically name all of the impairments that are covered.[7]

The protection provided by the ADA is protection from discrimination, as with other civil rights legislation. However, as the Civil Rights Division of the Department of Justice confirms, "Religious organizations and entities controlled by religious organizations have no obligations under the ADA."[8] People with disabilities have benefited enormously from ADA requirements that public spaces and educational institutions be opened to them, yet discrimination against people with disabilities still is deeply embedded in many social and religious practices.

Although the minority group model of disability is useful in many contexts, it is not always a natural fit for understanding or responding to human experiences. As theologian John Swinton points out, "There is nothing amongst the various impairments that people have which gives them a unified identity as 'disabled.' A person who is blind may have nothing at all in common with a person who has an intellectual disability. What holds them together as a unified group is this common experience of oppression, exclusion and injustice."[9] As we will see particularly in Chapter 7, this means that ecclesial responses to disability may function very differently as individual congregations seek to respond to the particular needs of specific groups of people with disabilities.

With any definition of disability, a tension emerges between the experience of people with disabilities as a stigmatized group and the reality that all human beings are limited and finite and require help and support from their families and communities. Theologian Deborah Creamer, in a 2015 lecture on disability, contrasts two images of disability. One is "disability as a neglected minority experience" and the other is "disability as a common, unsurprising, and 'normal' experience."[10] Both of these characterizations are accurate: disability is a normal, widespread experience that gives rise to often-ignored exclusion and discrimination.

Disability should not be ignored; as poet and DeafBlind activist John Lee Clark writes, "For disabled poets, my best advice is to write about disability. Or, rather, let disability, as part of your life, appear in your work. Disability is everywhere. It is, in fact, universal, for to be human is to be disabled. The only reason some people don't think of themselves as disabled is because most things out there are designed to accommodate their type of body and not other types."[11] While Clark can argue that disability is universal because nobody (literally, no body) can conform to a cultural ideal of total physical and psychological and intellectual capability and power, this reality of universal finitude does not erase the experiences associated with disability. One risk with this approach is that the social and political injustices people with disabilities experience are effaced. Craig Satterlee, a homiletician and Lutheran bishop who is also blind, argues that people should "avoid trivializing disability by making it a universal experience: 'She cannot walk and I cannot play piccolo. We all have our disabilities.' "[12] Echoing this position, Reynolds argues, "Claiming that 'we are all disabled' is only a partial truth; it overlooks the concrete forms of physical and emotional suffering that may accompany certain impairments and also sweeps away the realities of exclusion and oppression faced by persons whose impairments preclude participation in a world designed by and for non-disabled people."[13] Any religious response to or analysis of disability must balance these two realities: disability is common and it is also deeply stigmatized.

As should not surprise us given these varying analyses, Davis argues that disability is an "unstable category."[14] Impairment is a complicated concept, and as he argues, it relies upon a normative concept of an able-bodied self against which a disabled body is measured.[15] Clearly, disability is not a binary category, where a person either is able-bodied or has a disability. In addition, a shift in context may render a person who functions perfectly well under one set of circumstances impaired or disabled in another situation. A Deaf person whose first language is American Sign Language (ASL), finding himself in a room full of people who are fluent in ASL, is not impaired; however, he might be impaired when among a room of hearing people who expect him to function as a hearing person. A person's body may also function differently from one day to the next; a chronic pain condition, for instance, may be kept under control most of the time but flare up and become disabling without much notice. This means that attention to the specific experiences and needs of any one person or group is essential for formulating any meaningful response to the needs of people with disabilities and that theories of disability must also respond to the lived experiences of people experiencing disability.

Disability Theology

If disability is an unstable category, what is disability theology? It is, first of all, a theology of liberation. Gustavo Gutiérrez, a Catholic theologian and Dominican priest from Peru, wrote his best-known book, *A Theology of Liberation*, after serving very poor communities in the slums of Lima, Peru. He argues that God has a preferential option for the poor, grounding this position in the biblical texts. He writes, "In the first place, *liberation* expresses the aspirations of oppressed peoples and social classes, emphasizing the conflictual aspect of the economic, social, and political process which puts them at odds with wealthy nations and oppressive classes. … At a deeper level, *liberation* can be applied to an understanding of history. Humankind is seen as assuming conscious responsibility for its own destiny."[16] People with disabilities are among those who are economically, socially, politically, and religiously marginalized, and the theological claims of liberation theology serve as a basis for theology of disability. Analysis of disability as a category of human experience with religious import, and a categorization that has been used to oppress, makes disability theology a liberation theology.

Although Gutiérrez does not specifically write about disability in his description of liberation theology, he had firsthand experience with disability. As a young person he was confined to bed for six years with osteomyelitis, a bone disease, and remains somewhat impaired.[17] Gutiérrez reflects in a 2003 interview,

> I learned a lot about hope and joy when I was young. From the age of 12 to 18 I had osteomyelitis and was confined to bed. There certainly were reasons for discouragement, but also very present was the gift of hope that came to me through prayer, reading, family and friends. Later my parishioners in Lima would also teach me volumes about hope in the midst of suffering, and this is when I decided to write a book about Job. Hope is precisely for the difficult moments.[18]

One hope expressed in theologies of disability is for the transformation of religious communities into the kind of sustaining presence Gutiérrez describes.

Despite the experience of routine economic, social, political, and religious marginalization, people with disabilities have long been present in Christian religious communities. Their stories are richly represented in the biblical texts and the traditions of the church. Clark argues about the contributions and presence of people with disabilities, "We disabled people have always shaped the world around us, and our fingerprints on every aspect of life cannot be removed. To remove our presence and influence on American culture is to remove American culture. It would be a totally different world without us, as it would be without any other minority community."[19] The same is true of the church; thus, disability theology is not only a theology of liberation, but a theology of retrieval. To assert that the body of Christ is made up of the nonimpaired would be not only prejudiced but false. Yet, churches populated by well-meaning religious people do this all the time, effacing the presence and contributions and leadership of people with disabilities, while simultaneously failing to create opportunities for people with disabilities to worship, lead, and become faithful participants in congregations.

John Swinton argues,

> Disability theology begins with the recognition that people with disabilities have been at best a minority voice in the development of Christian theology and practice and at worst have been completely silenced within the conversation. In listening to such voices and reflecting on the life experiences of people with disabilities, it hopes to re-think and recalibrate aspects of theology and practice that serve to exclude or to misrepresent the human experience of disability.[20]

He emphasizes that disability theology is ecumenical and cross-disciplinary, building on insights from a variety of traditions and constructive disciplines.

Disability theology, then, seeks to raise and explore, and eventually to answer, questions about the meaning of disability for Christians. A theology of disability affirms the value of people with disabilities, critiques the social and religious practices that diminish their well-being, and argues for justice for people with disabilities in the church: in its theology, its preaching, its lived practices, and its self-understanding.

Personal Experiences

My own interest in disability theology began during graduate school, when I was reading and writing about the work of theologian Paul Tillich. Tillich suggests in sermons on healing and in his *Systematic Theology* that people with mental illness are choosing that illness and that salvation is healing. He writes in one sermon, "People [in the United States] are fleeing into a situation where others must take care of them, where they exercise power through weakness or where they create an imaginary world in which it is nice to live as long as real life does not touch them. Don't underestimate this temptation."[21] He valorizes the experience of health, arguing, "Health in the ultimate sense of the word, health as identical with salvation, is life in faith and love."[22] Perhaps his own deeply traumatic experience during World War I shaped Tillich's claim that people with mental illness are choosing to be ill (and could then presumably choose *not* to be ill). However, when I first read this, I found his argument deeply unsettling; a family member was struggling with significant depression, and the dissonance between what I saw of that experience and Tillich's analysis troubled me.

Eventually I began to read theologians of disability. Many years later, my own bodily experience has helped illuminate for me the complexity of experiences of disability. There is a popular principle among disability rights activists: *nothing about us without us.* This means that engaging in policy changes and analysis of disability without the ongoing participation of people who live with disabilities is profoundly misguided. Thus, there is a legitimate question for anyone writing about disability: what is your own connection to this issue? My answer to that question is that I am not, precisely, a person with a disability nor am I able-bodied.

In my late thirties, after about five years of decreasing mobility and increasing chronic pain, I was diagnosed with hip dysplasia. Ironically, the diagnoses came as I was developing the proposal for this book; as I thought through the structure and focus of the book, I learned about my own impairment. As I wrote, I prepared for and underwent and recovered from the initial joint replacement surgery, one of at least two, and perhaps more in the future as the current prosthetic joints age. I had been an avid runner, but stopped running when it became too painful. Eventually it became too difficult to even walk a mile. At my worst point I could not walk across my fairly small campus from the cafeteria back to my office without stopping to rest so that I could give my body a break from the pain. My colleagues grew accustomed to sitting with me until I was ready to walk again.

What did the experience teach me? Certainly, it underscored the reality that human bodies are limited, finite, and fragile. After my first surgery I was in a great deal of pain for several weeks. I was on crutches or using a walker for about a month, and used a cane for weeks after that. I was on "total hip precautions" for six months, which limited my ability to bend, cross my legs, and engage in activity that might dislodge the hip prosthetic from its socket.[23] When I first came home from the hospital and for weeks afterward, bathing was a many-step ritual. I had to maneuver very carefully into the shower with my crutches, I had an incision to protect from the water, and I had to sit on a shower chair because I could not stand unsupported. It reminded me of the first few newborn baths I gave to my children; nothing is more slippery or delicate or precious than a wet infant, but a brand new hip joint feels vulnerable in a similar way. I complained to my partner that bathing made me feel like a baby, an adult caregiver, and an elderly person all at once.

Prior to this experience, even as my mobility declined, I knew but also did not know that the sort of everyday competence I took for granted as a mostly able-bodied adult, competence that my doctor and I hope I will be able to return to for at least a while, is an illusion. I knew intellectually but had not actually absorbed the truth that human beings are limited and that human bodies are not predictable or reliable, and also that in that experience of vulnerability and impairment is another truth: the normative way of being is not the only way. I had to navigate not only the changes to my own body but the changes to my identity, and I had to figure out how and when to disclose those changes.

The problem of having to categorize my experience helped me see the ways in which, as Davis says, the category "disability" is unstable. If disability were a simple binary category, it would be clear to me that as a non-able-bodied person, I must be disabled. But I also can see that I have not experienced some of the more profound social consequences of disability: I have not, to my knowledge, been denied a job or an educational experience or (as we will discuss more in Chapter 4) control over my own reproductive capacities because of my bodily impairment. I have not been prevented by architectural barriers from entering a restaurant or found myself unable to use restroom facilities that are inaccessible. No one suggested I was impaired because of my sinful nature, and the general consensus is that I should more or less recover. From this limited experience of disability, I have been grateful for the many disability experts, biblical scholars, theologians, religious leaders, and laypeople whose work has helped me to more fully consider disability as a religious phenomenon.

Overview of This Book

Chapter 2, "Fruitful Reading of Scripture," develops a biblical hermeneutic for analyzing biblical texts that discuss disability, from both the Hebrew Bible and the New Testament. Chapter 3, "Self, Faith, and Christ," puts Martin Luther's little-known teaching on suicide into conversation with John Swinton's work on dementia, and investigates constructs of faith and salvation for people whose mental health or cognitive capabilities might seem to cut them off from Christian community. In Chapter 4, "Feminism Reproductive Rights and Disability," I take up the problematic issue of reproductive rights for people with disabilities juxtaposed with the profoundly troubling data on termination of pregnancies after diagnosis of fetal disability. Chapter 5, "Recognizing Voices, Honoring Testimony," describes the work of four religious leaders living with disability, and discusses their respective experiences of call, exclusion, and service. In Chapter 6, "Disability in the Contemporary Church," we will revisit the critique of the American Lutheran Church offered by Nancy Eiesland, examine the current position on disability of three mainline denominations, and investigate current practices in theological education. In Chapter 7, "Congregations and Ministry for People with Disabilities," I profile three contemporary congregations that have developed ministries for people with disabilities, and develop a set of best-practice recommendations. Finally, Chapter 8, "What, Then, of God?," examines John Swinton's overview of various theologies of disability and explores what disability theology might reveal to practicing Christians about the nature of God and Christian religious life.

CHAPTER TWO

Fruitful Reading of Scripture

Introduction

The Bible is the most central text to Christian theology, and thus is also central to any Christian understanding of disability. Hebrew Bible scholar Rebecca Raphael, who describes herself as a "late-deafened adult,"[1] asks rhetorically, "why study disability, and why study it in the Bible? Here are my short answers: because disability is a major human experience, and because the Bible contains the mother-lode of disability representation in Western culture."[2] The goal of this chapter is not only to study constructs of disability in the Bible but also to formulate and apply a hermeneutic that prioritizes some texts as more constructive than others for creating a liberating Christian understanding of disability.

Thus, our answers to Raphael's second question are somewhat different than hers. Disability *is* a major human experience. Why study disability in the Bible? To formulate and proclaim a reading of the Bible that recognizes people with disabilities as full participants in the message of the gospel. In order to read the Bible as a text that offers liberation to people with disabilities, Christians must engage in critical reflection on both the Bible and the standard Christian interpretation of the Bible, and must analyze the concept of disability and how it functions as a social and religious category.

Why is it a complicated task to read the Bible as a text of liberation of and for people with disabilities? In short, the Bible does not offer its readers a set of clear, unambiguous passages affirming the social and religious equality of people with disabilities. Far from it; as we will see, strong arguments could be made both for and against disability as a divine punishment for sin, and both for and against the full inclusion of people with disabilities in their religious communities as members and leaders of congregations. The Christian tradition does not have a unified history of supporting the liberation of people living with disabilities or of people from any other marginalized group;

it is a complex and diverse tradition with a sometimes very problematic history of affiliations with social and political power.

In the introduction to *Liberation Theologies of the United States*,[3] humanist scholar of religion Anthony Pinn argues, "while religious discourse buttressed oppressive activities such as the destruction of native populations and the enslavement of Africans, oppressed communities also made use of religion to critique and challenge this abuse."[4] This observation—that Christianity can be, and has been, used both to oppress and to challenge oppression—is true not only for native populations and enslaved African Americans but also for people with disabilities. Christian scripture, along with Christian theology and practice, can be used to marginalize or to affirm the equality of people living with disabilities.[5]

This is not only a theoretical problem, but one that has far-reaching implications for everyday religious practice. As homiletician Kathy Black observes, "The problem ... is that Christian tradition and the Bible itself are very ambiguous on [the topic of disability], and clergy end up conveying mixed and often confusing, contradictory messages—in pastoral care settings and in preaching."[6] Preaching has an effect on the religious beliefs of the congregation. The interpretive choices individual Christians, and Christian communities and leaders, make with respect to these texts can shape the religious life of churches and the individual experiences of many people with disabilities.

Presuming we stipulate up front the inherent value of people living with disabilities and thus the necessity of inclusive churches, how should we read Scripture? Theologian Thomas Reynolds is blunt in his description of his approach to biblical interpretation: "[B]ecause the Bible is ambiguous on the account of disability, this means becoming cautiously selective as interpreters, choosing certain themes over and/or against less favorable alternatives, explicit in providing warrants for our selections vis-à-vis their consistency with other biblical texts, themes, and norms as well as with our own present experience, sociocultural context, and general knowledge base."[7] This means that Christians seeking to take issues of disability seriously as part of their Christian practice must be prepared to reflect critically on the Bible, and—as all readers do, whether or not they realize it—to privilege some texts as more applicable to guiding Christian life than others. The Bible is a multivocal text, reflective of cultural and religious norms during the various periods of its composition and transcription. This does not mean the Bible is not the word of God; it means that Christians are required to, as Reynolds argues, read the Bible thoughtfully and critically. Some biblical texts are more suited than others for creating a church that regards people with disabilities as full members of the body of Christ.

What are the limits to a disability-affirming hermeneutic? Rebecca Raphael is straightforward about the difficulties of generating a disability-positive reading of the Bible as a whole:

> To read positively [with respect to disability] when this clearly violates what we can know about the text and its world strikes me as a breach of intellectual ethics for the sake of comfort, and in the long run, this is not even comfortable. It would … efface both the historical representation of disability in the Hebrew Bible, and also the historical experience of disabled persons who have undergone signification by interpreters of this text. There is a point beyond which deploring the past becomes a fruitless indulgence; but this effacement would occur in the present, for which I am partly responsible.[8]

Thus, we should not shy away from recognizing that the social context of the biblical text differs significantly from our own and that in interpreting the Bible we will make and use normative claims developed from the Christian scriptural tradition that will critique the text itself. Raphael continues, "I believe that disability studies can contribute a critical mode to the Bible. There is much more work to be done simply analyzing disability in the Bible and its cognate literatures."[9] This project of interpretation, like other critical, reflective readings of the Bible, seeks to provide Christians a strategy for proclaiming the gospels as liberating texts, in this case for people with disabilities. Thus, the claim of this chapter is not that the Bible affirms the equality and well-being of people with disabilities, full stop. It is that Christians can, and should, approach the biblical texts with the intention of living out their Christian faith with respect to people with disabilities, and should be honest about the difficulty and complexity of that process. However, Christians can also affirm that the gospel message remains one of love and liberation for all people, including people with disabilities.

Identifying Problems

One very problematic and common reading of the Bible for people with disabilities is what theologian of disability Nancy Eiesland calls the "sin-disability conflation."[10] This problem has two facets. She writes, "The persistent thread within the Christian tradition has been that disability denotes an unusual relationship with God and that the person with disabilities is either divinely blessed or damned: the defiled evildoer or the spiritual superhero."[11] One reason for this conflation is that the Bible does include texts that suggest that disability is a punishment from God, that disability is a mark of sin, and that people with disabilities ought to be excluded from religious leadership positions.[12] However, the Bible also includes texts rejecting the connection between disability and sin, and many texts instructing Christians to form communities grounded in love and inclusion. Choosing to impute particular sin or particular holiness to people with disabilities, then, is not simply reading the Bible, but selecting and adhering to a reading that is influenced by stigmas about disability.

At first blush, the idea of people with disabilities as divinely blessed seems encouraging enough. Why is a positive stereotype as problematic as a negative one? While characterizing disability as a mark of holiness or divine favor may seem preferable to attributing disability to sin or evil, it is still a flawed hermeneutic. Putting people with disabilities on a spiritual pedestal ignores their individual experiences and pushes them into the role of being examples for other people's religious growth, rather than recognizing them as human beings in their own right, each with his or her individual relationship to God. This strategy may solve the problem of connecting disability with sin, but it is not necessarily compassionate, nor does it recognize the agency of the person living with a disability. The impact of this approach is to dehumanize and minimize the agency of people with disabilities; whether disability is seen as a curse or punishment from God or as a blessing, the individual with a disability is prevented from being recognized as an individual human being in relationship with God. Instead, he or she is reduced to his or her disability.

Another closely related interpretive strategy that can be harmful to people with disabilities is the uncritical repetition of biblical metaphors about disability, especially in ecclesial settings. Again, the problem is the use of the body or experience of a person with disabilities for the religious edification of others. Theologian Amos Yong observes, "In the ancient world, the disability metaphors communicated successfully to non-disabled people only because of the presumed correlation that existed between outward forms and inward realities. ... [B]lindness as a spiritual condition only makes sense because literal blindness refers to the incapacity to see and understand things clearly and make one's way about the world."[13] Metaphors equating impairment with lack of capacity to know God or lack of faith are exclusionary for people with disabilities and unnecessary for preaching the gospel or understanding the experience of faith.

Developing a Hermeneutic: Black and Yong

What are the challenges of reading the Bible as a liberating text for people with disabilities? How does one remain faithful to the biblical text but reject texts that harm people with disabilities? What does such a hermeneutic look like, and how does it work in practice? To begin with, two central teachings derived from Scripture can guide us. First, *every human being is created in the image of God and is a beloved child of God*. One important implication of this doctrine is that people with disabilities are agents, recognized by God as valuable in their own right and not simply as object lessons for others. Second, *God wants justice for God's beloved children*. This means that not only are people living with disabilities entitled to equal consideration and status within the Christian community, but that God's envisioned and forthcoming kingdom, and the community of the church, cannot persist in practices of harmful exclusion or false claims conflating disability and sin. These two hermeneutic principles provide interpreters with the means to interpret the biblical text as liberating for people with disabilities. Of these many interpreters, two key thinkers have influenced my approach in this chapter: Kathy Black, whose 1996 book, *A Healing Homiletic: Preaching and Disability*, remains influential, and Amos Yong, whose 2011 book, *The Bible, Disability, and the Church*, provides a reading counter to what he calls the "normate" perspective from which the Bible is often interpreted.

What is at stake for modern people with disabilities when individuals, pastors, and religious communities interpret the Bible? Black argues that biblical interpretation has significant impact on the beliefs of typical Christians: "How we preach the healing texts contributes greatly to the theology and general attitude that laypeople have toward persons with disabilities in general. Our interpretation of these texts also contributes to the exclusion of persons with disabilities from most of our churches today."[14] Black sees a marked difference between Jesus's ministry and contemporary religious approaches to disability. She argues that Jesus's approach to people with disabilities he encountered was to enable them to be "full participants in their religious, secular, and domestic spheres."[15] However, this liberating model has not held sway; Black observes that since the period of Jesus's lifetime and the formation of what is now the Christian church, "the manner in which homileticians have preached these texts [of Jesus's healings] is often oppressive to people with disabilities. Intentional or not, the end result is exclusion and alienation. The liberating effects of Jesus' ministry have somehow become lost. ... The theologies and language used in our sermons often affects the disability community in a way that is the reverse of what is intended."[16] There are two important points here: One, Jesus's original practices have been misused to marginalize people with disabilities within Christian communities. Two, this marginalization also exists outside the church. We will explore these realities and their religious implications throughout this book.

Black identifies several principles of biblical interpretation for developing a hermeneutic that rejects marginalization of people with disabilities. Like Yong, Black rejects the use of stigmatizing biblical metaphors in modern-day sermons. She also emphasizes the importance of recognizing the agency of biblical figures with disabilities, the interdependence of all people upon each other, and the problem of conflating disability with sin or punishment, and finally, she provides a useful distinction between the concepts of cure and healing. Black argues that *"Cure* is the elimination of at least the symptoms if not the disease itself. *Healing,* on the other hand, has many meanings attached to it. ... One aspect of healing entails finding some sense of meaning in the midst of one's situation, some sense of well-being in spite of the illness."[17] Thus, Jesus's acts of healing are more socially and spiritually nuanced than cures. Preaching, Black says, too often focuses on the idea of cure instead of healing, missing crucial aspects of the biblical texts and further alienating people whose disabilities are not in need of curing.

Black also firmly rejects the idea that God punishes people with illness or impairment, and thus that disability is a sign of sin. Analyzing the healing story in Mark 2, she writes,

> Homileticians and commentators vary in their approach to this text.... . Many encourage preachers to focus on the perceived relationship between sin and sickness, which then requires forgiveness before healing is possible. ... To preach that the reason people get the flu is because God is angry with them, let alone to put forth the notion that once the flu is gone God has forgiven our sins, is beyond absurd.[18]

Black's approach to biblical interpretation and to preaching thus provides a hermeneutical model that affirms the value of people with disabilities while also taking the biblical texts seriously as Scripture.

Amos Young identifies himself as a theologian, rather than a biblical scholar, and sets out the agenda of identifying and rejecting the biases of ableism when interpreting the Bible. He regards this as religious work, and describes himself as "proposing a new portrait for what it means to be the whole people of God that values and is inclusive of people with disabilities."[19] Yong makes a set of claims about this portrait: Like Black, Yong argues that the Bible can be a liberating gospel for people with disabilities. Also like Black, he emphasizes recognizing the agency of people with disabilities in biblical narratives, rather than assigning them the role of object lesson for able-bodied people. He reminds his readers to consider the social aspect of disability, shifting the identification of the problems associated with disability from the body of the individual person to the unjust structures of the society in which he or she lives. Finally, Yong argues for a Christological reading of healing narratives, arguing that the key to understanding them is not the physical cure of the person who is healed, but the redemptive and salvific power of Christ.

One important interpretive issue that Yong identifies is the tension between developing a liberating reading of the Bible for people with disabilities while recognizing the common and deep-rooted belief that God is in total control of human lives and human experience, and afflicts people with disabilities as punishment or to teach human beings a lesson. Yong argues that this is "the heart of the problem for any traditional theology of disability."[20] Together, Black and Yong, along with a host of other biblical scholars and theologians, will guide our reading of the Bible.

Biblical Texts and Key Hermeneutical Principles

Recall that the first interpretive principle I proposed above is "Every human being is created in the image of God and is a beloved child of God." This doctrine of the *Imago Dei* is most clearly articulated in Genesis 1:26–31. There is no explicit mention of disability in this text.[21] Human beings are first planned, then created; God says in verse 26 to the heavenly host, "Let us make humankind in our image, according to our likeness." Human beings are distinct from, and have responsibility for, the animals of both sea and land, both wild and domesticated. While classical Western philosophy has identified the human rational capacity as the feature that distinguishes humankind from other forms of life, in this biblical text God establishes human identity as a result of human resemblance to God, rather than any particular capacity. Nor does God suggest that some human beings are more fully capable of living out the image of God than others; verse 27 emphasizes that both male and female human beings are created in the image of God. God blesses human beings and instructs them to reproduce, and offers them a brief description of their place in the world vis-à-vis the other creatures God has created: everything with the breath of life, and every green living thing, has been provided for the human beings to have dominion over.

What might this mean for people with disabilities? Theologian Thomas Reynolds asks rhetorically, "Do persons with disabilities signify a lack of wholeness, a deficiency that blights the image of God? Emphatically, no! Every human being has the image of God in common, even as it is expressed in variety and difference."[22] There are at least two possible implications of a full affirmation of all human beings, including human beings with disabilities, as created in the image of God and therefore beloved children of God.

First, Reynolds argues that our thinking about bodies and about disability is often shaped by what he calls the "cult of normalcy." He argues that in each society, some ideals of form and function are valued over others; this is a social construct rather than something innately true about the bodies being evaluated. The cult of normalcy is "a set of rituals trained upon demarcating and policing the borders of a 'normal' way of being. ... The cult of normalcy deals with bodily variations by rendering them pathological and deficient vis-à-vis reference points of power and privilege."[23] In other words, a person with a body that does not fit into the constructed social ideal of a "good" or "capable" body becomes socially marginalized.

The notion of the *Imago Dei* provides the means to problematize this "cult of normalcy" and helps us reject the false notion that only people with "perfect" bodies (or minds or psyches) are created in the image of God. This claim is illusory and it is sinful. What Reynolds calls the cult of normalcy runs contrary to the biblical description of God's creative act in Genesis 1. God affirms human beings as created in God's image. God does not specify that being in the image of God requires that a person be, for example, a neurotypical adult untouched by aging or any bodily impairment, capable of "normal" physical tasks and without physical or intellectual vulnerability. Although human beings do, in fact, fail to recognize the image of God in many of their fellow human beings, we should be able to recognize this failure and subsequent rejection of others' dignity and value as sinful. The sin, then, is not in the bodies of the people living with disabilities, but in the social response to them inasmuch as that response stigmatizes and marginalizes some of God's children.

Prophetic Texts

The second biblical norm I offered above is "God wants justice for God's beloved children." This claim is central to liberation theologies and deeply embedded in the Hebrew Bible as well as the New Testament. Numerous Hebrew Bible texts form the foundation for Christian calls for inclusivity, outreach to the marginalized, and a church that regards each person as important. People with disabilities are consistently depicted as being moved by God from the margins to the center. Among the prophetic texts that specifically speak to God's active response to people with impairment are Jeremiah 31:7–9, Zephaniah 3:19–20, Micah 4:6–7, and Isaiah 35:5–7. These texts offer background for a full understanding of Jesus's healing miracles, complex narratives that have been interpreted by Christians in a variety of ways, some liberating and some re-stigmatizing of people with disabilities. Related to this claim that God wants justice for God's children is a rejection of the belief that disability is a punishment for sin, is caused by sin, or is an indicator of impurity or a sign that a person with a disability *should* be relegated to the margins of society or the church.

First, let us take up the Hebrew Bible prophetic texts that describe God's actions toward people who are on the margins of society. While the texts from Jeremiah, Micah, Zephaniah, and Isaiah are not identical, there are shared themes and claims about God's forthcoming restructuring of society. In each case, God's intention of collecting together some people on the social margins is proclaimed. The prophets emphasize God's act of restoration to the community, rather than God's intervention to change the structure or function of people's bodies. Sometimes people with disabilities, referred to with the now-jarring term "the lame," are juxtaposed with other people whose social or physical status makes them vulnerable. In each case, God proclaims their future social restoration.

In Jeremiah 31:8 the scattered "remnant" whom God will gather is varied: "See, I am going to bring them from the land of the north, and gather them from the farthest parts of the earth, among them the blind and the lame, those with child and those in labor." Clearly, here impairment is the issue, as pregnant women, those who are blind or whose mobility is impaired, and those who are actively laboring are all one category. The prophet speaks about God's intention of collecting the people, consoling them as they weep, providing water, and thus restoring those who are impaired to the community. What is of concern to God is the marginalization of some people for the benefit of others.

Similarly, Zephaniah 3:19 reads, "I will deal with all your oppressors at that time. And I will save the lame and gather the outcast, and I will change their shame into praise and renown in all the earth." The oppressors of the whole community are God's concern, but those who are impaired and others who have been unjustly cast out are singled out for a particular promise: they will, in a future promised by God, be raised up. In modern language, God rejects oppression of and by the people of Israel and promises through the prophet to reverse the stigma imposed on those who are impaired and others who are marginalized.

Micah 4:6–7 involves a similar proclamation:

6 On that day, says the Lord, I will assemble the lame and gather those who have been driven away, and those whom I have afflicted. 7 The lame I will make the remnant, and those who were cast off, a strong nation; and the Lord will reign over them in Mount Zion now and for evermore.

Here God is depicted as reversing social exclusion of three sorts: those who are impaired, those who have been driven out (presumably for other reasons), and those whom God has afflicted with some experience that has led to their exclusion. God promises to make the impaired into the "remnant," the members of the community who remain after a crisis.

In Isaiah 35:5–7, we have a similar text, but one that is problematic for several reasons. The text reads,

> Then the eyes of the blind shall be opened, and the ears of the deaf unstopped; 6 then the lame shall leap like a deer, and the tongue of the speechless sing for joy. For waters shall break forth in the wilderness, and streams in the desert; 7 the burning sand shall become a pool, and the thirsty ground springs of water; the haunt of jackals shall become a swamp, the grass shall become reeds and rushes.

The prophet lists four kinds of bodily impairment (blindness, deafness, impairment of mobility, and impairment of speech) and compares those bodily experiences to dry wilderness, dry desert, burning sands, thirsty ground, and dry grasslands where jackals live. While the text provides a series of images of restoration, here the bodies of people with disabilities and not their social marginalization is the focus of God's action. This is an example of a text that provides an unfortunate opportunity to reiterate rather than reject stigma toward the bodies of people with disabilities. Incautious affirmation of this text would fall exactly into the traps that Black and Yong warn us against; instead, the text must be read critically and recognized as one that, if preached without sufficient contextualization, runs the risk of sinfully mischaracterizing the place of people with disabilities in Christian community. God wants justice for God's beloved children, and in the modern world we are positioned to recognize that this justice comes not from reshaping the bodies of people with disabilities, but from reshaping the social and even physical world around them to provide access and welcome.

Sin and Disability

In John 9, Jesus has one of the longest engagements with a person with a disability depicted in the New Testament, when he heals the man born blind. It is a rich and complex text. Jesus and his disciples see a man, they discuss the religious implications of the man's blindness (including Jesus's proclamation of one of the "I am" statements distinctive of John's Gospel), and then Jesus performs a healing ritual on the man's body and instructs him to go wash. The man attracts the attention of members of the community who are now confused about who he is, and he speaks on his own behalf. The man is twice asked to offer an assessment of Jesus's identity; his response is rejected by the religious leaders while his status as a sinner is reiterated, and he eventually confesses his faith directly to Jesus. Jesus makes an analogy between blindness and the religious leaders' lack of faith, and the passage ends.

Biblical scholar Colleen Grant argues that one of the most compelling features of this narrative is the "well-developed character" of the man whom Jesus encounters. She writes, "[D]espite his anonymity, the man born blind comes alive in this healing narrative. ... He appears not simply as a broken figure in need of compassion and healing but as a person in his own right. We are able to get to know him as a thoughtful, brave, amusing, but above all, ordinary person."[24] This text offers a robust opportunity to explore the agency of a person with a disability; as Grant notes, Jesus disappears for 28 verses, leaving the man whom he has healed as the focus of that part of the text.[25] Black's strategy of emphasizing the personhood of people with disabilities in the Bible is important in interpreting this text.

There are several other key theological issues in this narrative. One is the disciples' question in 9:2 about whose sin is the source of the man's blindness: his, or his parents'? Jesus replies that neither is the case. Grant argues, following Rudolf Bultmann, that the connection between sin and disability is not wholly dismissed by Jesus, but only set aside in this particular instance.[26] However, Jesus's response to the disciples provides a powerful reminder to the reader that disability cannot be assumed to be a punishment for sin; in this case, he argues in 9:3, the man "was born blind so that God's works might be revealed in him." Jesus goes on to reiterate the theme of light and revelation so central to the gospel; echoing John 1:5, he tells the disciples in 9:5, "As long as I am in the world, I am the light of the world." This language, as Grant points out, is echoed in verse 9, when after his healing the man must reassert his identity to the community, including the religious leaders.[27]

The man's neighbors have clearly made a set of assumptions that the text disrupts: they have discounted the man's personhood and his agency, his capacity to speak on his own behalf and to provide religious testimony. They have also done something that still happens to people with disabilities: they have conflated his blindness with his identity. Once he is able to see, they literally cannot recognize him as the same person. This mistake, both in the context of the narrative and when it is made in the present day, clearly interferes with the community's ability to value, empathize with, and trust the person who lives with a disability. His physical capabilities have changed, but his identity has not. The man's neighbors investigate the situation, and then the religious leaders of the community, who are concerned about Jesus's status and identity, ask him in verse 17, "What do you say about him? It was your eyes he opened." Here he is asked to tell them who Jesus is; seemingly, he is now regarded as a reliable witness. However, his reply, that Jesus is a prophet, does not satisfy them and although he was just moments before recognized as himself, suddenly his identity is questioned again. The leaders seek out his parents to ask whether he is really their son.

When his parents confirm his identity and then distance themselves from the growing controversy, the man becomes more confident both about Jesus's identity and his own capacity to speak. Instructed to give glory to God, which Grant identifies as a reminder to tell the truth,[28] he first says in verse 25 that he does not know whether Jesus is a sinner but can testify that Jesus opened his eyes. Then his understanding of Jesus begins to change as he reflects on his own experience. He says in 9:30–32,

> Here is an astonishing thing! You do not know where he comes from, and yet he opened my eyes. 31 We know that God does not listen to sinners, but he does listen to one who worships him and obeys his will. 32 Never since the world began has it been heard that anyone opened the eyes of a person born blind. 33 If this man were not from God, he could do nothing.

The magnitude of what has happened to him gives rise to a new understanding of Jesus. Not only is the man a reliable witness with the capacity to analyze his own experience, he exercises the agency that his community has demanded of him and his parents have stipulated he possesses.

The response of the religious leaders to the man's conviction is dramatic. They say in verse 34, "You were born entirely in sins, and are you trying to teach us?" and drive him out. They have mistaken his disability for evidence of sin, they have been unable to conceive of his having an identity apart from his disability, and they reject him as incapable of teaching not on the grounds of his blindness but on the grounds that his former blindness must exclude him from a position of authority.

The passage concludes with the man's second encounter with Jesus, who seeks him out. Jesus explains to the man that he is the Son of Man, and the man's response is to confess his faith. However, the narrative ends on a perplexing note: Jesus says, "I came into this world for judgment so that those who do not see may see, and those who do see may become blind." He tells the religious leaders in verse 41, "If you were blind, you would not have sin. But now that you say, 'We see,' your sin remains." What are we to make of this conclusion, where Jesus himself uses blindness as an analogy for lack of faith?

Theologian Jennie Weiss Block offers suggestions for avoiding the trap of reifying stigma in preaching: "Do not objectify the disabled person [in the biblical passage]. Instead, focus on their personal qualities or behavior or some other aspect of the story. Never describe the healing in a way that creates pity for the person with the disability. Do not reduce a person's experience of embodiment to a metaphor. Everyone has heard the metaphor about spiritual blindness a thousand times anyway!"[29] In this pericope, Jesus does offer a metaphor where actual blindness represents spiritual blindness. The text should not be excised, but in proclaiming the Bible and using it to develop a theological point of view, a church policy, or a deeper understanding of God, we can set this metaphor aside as unhelpful and outdated. Does it affirm the status of all human beings as made in the image of God? Does it emphasize God's desire for justice for those on the margins? Is it liberating? Not especially. Thus, it does not have to be the foreground of our understanding of disability or God's relationship to human beings living with disability.

Priesthood and Disability

Another particularly difficult biblical text, which has been written about extensively by biblical scholars interested in disability, is Leviticus 21:16–24. The text lays out conditions that render some priests ineligible for full participation in the ritual sacrifices within the Temple. The list of conditions in verses 18 through 20 is painfully precise:

> For no one who has a blemish shall draw near, one who is blind or lame, or one who has a mutilated face or a limb too long, 19 or one who has a broken foot or a broken hand, 20 or a hunchback, or a dwarf, or a man with a blemish in his eyes or an itching disease or scabs or crushed testicles.

Verses 22 and 23 clarify the limits of the exclusion and the rationale:

> He may eat the food of his God, of the most holy as well as of the holy. 23 But he shall not come near the curtain or approach the altar, because he has a blemish, that he may not profane my sanctuaries; for I am the Lord; I sanctify them.

How do interpreters invested in issues of disability respond to this description in the Bible of some impairments as "profaning" the sanctuary? Kathy Black, for one, interprets the text in its historical context, arguing, "Exclusion from the temple involved both the issue of needing boundaries for protection and the issue of purity or holiness. Nothing could defile the temple. For these reasons, Leviticus 21:17–23 forbids persons with disabilities from making offerings or going near the altar."[30] The idea that the presence and participation of a visibly impaired person could defile the religious ritual reads as harsh and stigmatizing to modern ears.

What was the historical origin of this restriction? Rebecca Raphael notes the parallels between the characteristics animals must have to be eligible for sacrifice on the altar and the specifications for the bodies of the human beings serving as priests. She argues,

> [T]he presence of animals allows us to infer a species criterion at work. The graver consequences for priestly blemish, compared to animal blemish, indicate a privileging of the human form. And the exclusion of dwarfs, hunchbacks, and those with uneven limbs reflects an underlying concept of "correct" stature and symmetry. Size and symmetry, although visible, are not simply visual phenomenon. They reflect a sense of right proportionality, one based on the non-disabled human male. If blemish is the opposite of wholeness, and the most obvious blemishes are the ones listed, then wholeness means a body with a smooth, symmetrical, unruptured surface, on a frame of the right species, gender, and size.[31]

The criteria for priestly participation in sacrifice, then, are aesthetic rather than moral. Inasmuch as the priest, like the sacrifice itself, was supposed to represent wholeness and perfection, the visual appearance of his body was considered important to the proper functioning of the ritual. As Yong argues, this realization is important in justifying setting aside these requirements: "Jewish interpreters have thus suggested that while there is an aesthetic criterion at work in this passage, it should be subordinated to the Hebrew Bible's emphasis on God's electing a poor and marginalized people for his own."[32] To Yong, the import of God seeking justice for God's beloved children is greater than the prescription of aesthetic perfection among the priests who serve God.

Biblical scholar Sarah Melcher takes up this text and asks, "Is the rhetorical intention of this passage to devalue certain individuals? What options are available to those who would interpret these passages?"[33] She reviews the ancient belief (not exclusive to ancient Jews, but common in the Near East) that impairment is a punishment from God.[34] She notes that verse 22, which permits a blemished priest to eat the food of God, indicates that the priest is not ritually impure, and like Raphael, she describes the parallels between animals appropriate for sacrifice and the physical specifications for priests.[35] Then Melcher asks, "Given the stigmatizing power of [this biblical text], what can biblical interpretation do to lessen that power without compromising the authority of the scriptural text?"[36] In other words, how can modern readers, Jewish or Christian, take the biblical text seriously but reject the idea that people with disabilities are somehow lesser members of the community, or are unfit for religious leadership?

Melcher advises,

> Although I would not recommend de-sacralizing texts, I do think we can desacralize stigma imbedded within them. Feminist interpretation and liberation approaches to Scripture have offered us ways to face prejudice in texts and to recast their influence. In this instance we are fortunate. Within Leviticus, Chapter 19 offers us a different paradigm. Leviticus 19:14 instructs us, "You shall not revile the deaf or put a stumbling block before the blind: you shall fear your God: I am the Lord." Further on, Leviticus 19:18b reminds us, "you shall love your neighbor as yourself: I am the Lord." ... One way to love our neighbors is to refuse to devalue them and resist using Scripture to justify our prejudice.[37]

This reading can help Christian interpreters avoid a pitfall some fall into when considering difficult passages in the Hebrew Bible, which goes something like this: "Those were Jewish laws that predated the grace of Christ. As Christians we don't need to live by the old covenant but the new one, so that rule doesn't matter." Jesus was not the lone light in a dark, disability-scorning world who single-handedly healed all and sundry in the face of Jewish opposition; in fact, Melcher's reading relies on other passages from Leviticus to desacralize the problematic parts of the text. Engaging in anti-Jewish rhetoric does no favors to Christians with or without disabilities and reiterates a longstanding and profoundly harmful anti-Semitic thread of Christian belief and practice.

Envisioning the Church

What models of an inclusive, diverse church do we have in Scripture? In I Corinthians 12, the Apostle Paul offers the Corinthian church a model for proper ecclesial relationships, which modern readers increasingly regard as a model for addressing problems of exclusion of people with disabilities from Christian congregations, and especially for the problem of disregarding or overlooking their gifts and leadership.[38] As theologian Brian Brock argues, "I Corinthians 12 has become a core text anchoring an emerging consensus about the theological definition of inclusion. This is no doubt the case because in it the Apostle Paul presents his most elaborated meditations on the theme of the body of Christ, developing an especially incisive description of the interpersonal dynamics of that body understood as a political entity."[39] The church at Corinth had, as we can discern from Paul's letter, some conflicts regarding the status of individual members; Brock argues that one central problem Paul was addressing was the conflation of worldly (i.e., extra-Christian) social status of various members with their status within the church.[40] Paul's response, in which he reproaches the congregation for this mistake, both affirms Jesus's rejection of human social hierarchies and provides a model for the flourishing of people with disabilities within Christian congregations.

Paul's invocation of the body as his model for the social relationships within the congregation should remind us of the cautions given by both Black and Yong against reiterating, especially in preaching, bodily metaphors found in the Bible that use disability as an example of rejection of God or failure to hear Jesus's message. Does Paul's invocation of the body fall into the category of problematic bodily metaphor, or does his language and imagery provide a constructive biblical model for inclusive congregations?

First, it is important to see Paul's language and imagery in context. Brock argues, "Tales of conversations between individual body parts were standard fare in the ancient world, as was their deployment to illumine aspects of political relationships."[41] Brock notes that Livy, Plato, Aristotle, Cicero, Seneca, and Epictetus all use this technique, so Paul was engaged in a kind of rhetoric that his readers may have heard before, and it reflects his status as an educated Greek-speaking person.[42] Even an unlettered person who had never encountered Plato would have had the advantage of being familiar with his or her own body, and with the core idea that each part of the body has a different but important function.

Given the existence of this trope, how does Paul's use of the metaphor of the body, where the human body is positioned to be analogous to the body of Christ, work in I Corinthians, and how can it illuminate the problem in the Corinthian church and reveal to us solutions to problems of exclusion or unjust social hierarchies we face in our own congregations? In other words, how can this passage from Paul be read in a way that is liberating for people with disabilities, and is constructive for congregations that wish to be inclusive?

Paul does three key things in this text. One, he argues that God the Spirit gives gifts to each person and that every role within the Christian community uses gifts provided by the Spirit. Two, he uses the metaphor of the human body to establish that each gift is necessary to the functioning of the community and that no gift or person can be neglected or excluded if the church is to function as God intended. Three, he explicitly rejects the hierarchical practices of the world outside the church, where some people are valued more than others, and reminds his readers that one purpose of the Christian community is to reverse these unjust social stratifications so that each person is equally a member of the body of Christ.

Paul writes in verses 7 through 11,

> 7 To each is given the manifestation of the Spirit for the common good. 8 To one is given through the Spirit the utterance of wisdom, and to another the utterance of knowledge according to the same Spirit, 9 to another faith by the same Spirit, to another gifts of healing by the one Spirit, 10 to another the working of miracles, to another prophecy, to another the discernment of spirits, to another various kinds of tongues, to another the interpretation of tongues. 11 All these are activated by one and the same Spirit, who allots to each one individually just as the Spirit chooses.

This argument emphasizes the universality of the work of the Spirit. *Each* person is given a particular gift, and the purpose of that gift is not self-aggrandizement or financial profit or personal fulfillment, but "the common good." Read with questions of disability in mind, we can conclude that every person—disabled or able-bodied—has been given gifts that will benefit the Christian community. Moreover, Paul provides a list of gifts. Although as modern people we can assume this list is not exhaustive of all possible gifts from God that might be used in a Christian community (where we might need leaders for youth or volunteers to help maintain the church's website or skilled community organizers), we should also note that none of the gifts presumes that the person's body functions according to narrow social ideals of what is "normal." A person with a disability could easily find herself the recipient of any of the gifts Paul lists, and as we expand that list to reflect the religious and social needs of communities in the twenty-first century, we can see that each person has gifts that can be useful within a religious community. Moreover, Paul is firm in arguing that the Holy Spirit distributes and activates these gifts; it is not up to the community to assign gifts or establish them, only to recognize and cultivate them for the flourishing of the whole church.

Paul's metaphor of the body raises an interesting potential problem for interpreters seeking a liberating reading of the Bible for people with disabilities. Paul's envisioned body that functions as a stand-in for the church as the body of Christ seems to be able-bodied. For instance, the eyes, ears, nose, hands, and feet (not to mention the head!) seem in his analogy all to be functioning in what Yong calls "normate" fashion. The eyes see; the ears hear. Where does this leave the reader of Paul who is blind or deaf? Both Yong and Black caution us against uncritically repeating biblical analogies that elevate able-bodied selves at the expense of bodies that are disabled.

Yong argues that "in the ancient Mediterranean context, these body parts [hands and feet, eyes and ears] are the nexuses through which human bodies interface and interact with the world. They are considered necessary because eyes see, ears hear, hands feel, and feet cross the external world."[43] We can affirm Paul's central meaning here—that all people have a function and purpose in the church community—while recognizing that some people interface with the world in nonnormative ways. People who are blind or deaf engage the world and communicate perfectly well; people with mobility or sensory impairments also cross the world and engage with their surroundings. Most people with intellectual disabilities, even if they do not have significant capacity for expressive language, can offer responses to the world in which they live and the people who surround them and care for them. Although on the surface Paul's metaphor reinforces normative expectations of bodies and their functioning, it would be a mistake to read his argument as exclusive of people with disabilities.

Indeed, in verses 22 through 25 Paul explicitly rejects the idea of rank-ordering people's gifts according to external benchmarks of importance or power. His discussion of weakness, indispensability, respectability, and honor requires some unpacking. He clearly rejects the idea that the "inferior members," those people in the congregation who seem to be weaker or less honorable, are actually less valuable than their co-congregants with higher social status. He argues that instead, within the context of the church, they are indispensible and regarded with "greater honor." In fact, he says, God has ordained that the body of Christ function this way as an equalizing force. The people who already have social status or honor do not need to have the church provide them with their due share of dignity; that is reserved for those who are devalued.

Here Paul provides a model for churches to respond to the discriminatory practices of the broader society against people with disabilities (and indeed, any marginalized people). The church should be a place where the gifts God has given to and revealed in each person are recognized and cultivated by the community. This is particularly the case for people whose gifts might be disregarded by the outside world because of their social status in a hierarchical society that does not see as God sees. As Yong argues, "[I]t is the responsibility of the whole body to end the stigmatization and marginalization of people with disabilities."[44] This is part of what it means to be the church.

Conclusions

The Bible offers innumerable rich and complex texts depicting the human experience of disability; we have discussed only a few. Some of these texts are easily understood and proclaimed as liberating for people with disabilities and offer constructive models for understanding ourselves and building just and welcoming religious communities. Some texts are deeply problematic, and have given rise to a Christian doctrine that excludes and stigmatizes people with disabilities, calling into question their personhood and their status as children of God. The Bible and the Christian tradition have the power to liberate but also the power to oppress. As modern people we have tools for interpretation that permit us to construct theological positions in keeping with God's love for and affirmation of all human beings, including people with disabilities. This hermeneutic of liberation is not fixed or complete but fluid and ongoing, and should be practiced with the same enthusiasm and seriousness of purpose that Christians have always brought to their reading of the gospel.

CHAPTER THREE

Self, Faith, and Christ: Questions of Suicide and Dementia

Introduction

About five years ago I taught a class on Lutheranism, and showed the 2003 film directed by Eric Till called *Luther*. The film is a biography of Luther, with some dramatic license taken, but on the whole reasonably historically sound, and well acted and directed. Two scenes were particularly gripping to my students: one where Luther is called to the home of a family whose adolescent son has ended his own life, and one where Luther preaches a rousing, affirming sermon to his congregation, making clear to the community, including the young man's parents, that the young man is in heaven. The grief of the family is palpable in the film: the mother's cry as her husband and her priest gently cradle her son's body after cutting him down from the beam from which he has hung himself is deep and sorrowful. The father turns to Luther and asks, "What does God say, Father, for suicide?"[1] Luther does not immediately reply, but retreats into his monk's cell and engages in an emotionally charged argument with the devil. Then he is depicted wresting a shovel from the gravedigger, who is protesting against the possibility of burying the young man in the Catholic cemetery because it is holy ground.

Luther begins to dig the young man's grave in the church's cemetery. While he is digging, a crowd gathers, and he speaks to them. Luther argues, "Some people say that according to God's justice, this boy is damned because he took his own life. I say he was overcome by the devil. Is this child any more to blame for the despair that overtook him than an innocent man who was murdered by a robber in the woods?"[2] He then buries the young man, slipping his own crucifix from around his neck and interring it with the young man's body. Later in the film Luther offers a sermon in which he makes the argument that rather than a God of anger and punishment, "we have a God of love." He encourages the congregation, including the young man's parents, to admit to the devil that they "deserve death and hell" but that instead Christ has provided them with salvation.[3] After we finished watching the film in class, a student asked, as students everywhere will do, "Did that really happen?" I had to confess I did not know, I began to read about Luther's teaching on suicide. The short answer to the student's question turns out to be, as the answer so often is, Yes and No and It's Very Complicated.

However vivid Luther's words are in these cinematic exhortations and in his real letters (as we will see below), his description of suicidal ideation as a struggle with the devil may not resonate today and may even further stigmatize people experiencing mental illness.[4] And yet Luther's teaching on suicide, expressed clearly in his letters of consolation, may also provide comfort and hope for people who are suicidal and their families, given his emphasis on God's overwhelming love. What good might these writings from Luther do for modern people who suffer, or whose loved ones suffer, from depression or other mental illness? Can Luther's writings be developed into an approach to pastoral care that is medically and scientifically responsible, and useful for modern Christians?[5]

One effective strategy for considering Luther's writing on suicide comes from an unexpected place: theological writing on dementia. Scottish theologian and healthcare professional John Swinton identifies dementia as an experience that, like suicidal ideation, poses questions to Christians about the persistence of selfhood, of eligibility for salvation, and of the efficacy of the love of God. He argues in his book *Dementia: Living in the Memories of God* that for persons experiencing dementia, Descartes's classic claim "I think, therefore I am" needs to be replaced with the theological claim "We are because God sustains us in God's memory."[6] Both those whose cognitive capabilities are diminishing because of dementia and their loved ones may hold deep spiritual concerns that the salvation status and the identity of the person with dementia as a child of God are endangered by the loss of memory. What is at issue is this: if a person has forgotten his or her own identity and any prior Christian faith, is salvation still possible? Many constructs of faith emphasize the participant's agency and belief, which may fade with dementia.

Similarly, the Christian tradition has long (although not uniformly) taught that people who end their lives—often as a result of what we now recognize as mental illness—have endangered or even forfeited their eternal salvation. Although the history of ecclesial and civil responses to suicide is complex, in the early modern period, when Luther lived, for both Roman

Catholics and Protestants the burial of the body of a person who had committed suicide was typically not a straightforward matter. This ambiguity of
status of the body reflects an ambiguity of the status of the soul; although
burial of the body was not generally held to control salvation, it was a sign
of the community's regard for the person's status in eternal life.[7] Thus, the
film *Luther* points the viewer to a genuine question within the tradition:
what can be made of a person who ends his or her own life?

Similar questions emerge, although perhaps more quietly, for people
whose identity is fading because of dementia. In both cases, those of people
who are suicidal and those of people who are experiencing dementia,
the cognitive or psychological status of the individual person is sometimes
thought to cancel out the meaning and efficacy of previous participation
in the Christian tradition. Although dementia is not identical with suicidal
depression, Swinton's analysis of the bodily and spiritual experiences of
persons with dementia suggests numerous fruitful possibilities for a reading
of Luther's letters of spiritual counsel.

This is not only an academic question. While working on a conference
paper that served as an early draft of this chapter, I happened to hear from
a philosophy professor who had seen the paper proposal; she shared a story
from her congregation. A man who was a member of her church community was experiencing dementia and he ended his own life. He had, earlier
in his life, expressed doubt that people who committed suicide went to
heaven. His widow and children were left in their grief with the knowledge
that he had been a good man and a faithful Christian, but also with terrible
doubt about his salvation. Their pastors and congregation members had
supported them in this loss and reminded them of the grace of God, but
their worry about their loved one's salvation lingered. The professor who
wrote asked whether she could share the paper proposal I had written
describing Luther's letters and Swinton's book, in the hopes that those resources would provide some means of comfort. I was both willing to be of
any help that I could and powerfully struck by the story. This question of
the relationship between cognition, illness, and salvation is not only a
sixteenth-century problem, and the two situations, dementia and suicidal
depression, may pose to us similar religious questions.

The social response to people with dementia is often grim. Swinton
describes language used to characterize people with dementia with dismay;
they are often spoken of as having lost their personhood, as being no longer
themselves, no longer present, or even functionally dead. For example, a
friend of Swinton's writes to tell him the all-too-common advice she has
gotten from an Alzheimer's care organization: she should divorce her husband and move on with her life. On another occasion, a nurse remarked

lightly to her that it was time to euthanize him.[8] Religious response is not necessarily better, especially when the person with dementia no longer has the capacity to express religious belief. Consider the importance to many Christians of Mark 16:16: "The one who believes and is baptized will be saved; but the one who does not believe will be condemned." It is not difficult to see why someone whose belief can no longer be expressed might be seen as having lost his or her salvation.

Swinton holds that, contrary to the view that a person's having forgotten God means all is lost, God is sufficiently powerful to remember, and love, the "vanishing self."[9] He argues, "[I]t is impossible to understand the full meaning of being a human person without first understanding who God is and where human beings stand in relation to God."[10] This position dovetails with the foundational Lutheran claim that salvation is by grace, through faith rather than as the result of human effort or merit. It also relies upon a robust account of God's compassion toward suffering human beings. Indeed, Swinton considers the words of Dietrich Bonhoeffer in presenting his position on God's care for those with dementia: "Only the suffering God can help."[11]

Swinton's analysis of the religious experience of people with dementia presents a robust theoretical basis for reconsidering Luther's pastoral response to those who are bereaved, those who are anxious and despondent, and particularly those whose loved ones have attempted or committed suicide. Although Luther did not have access to a modern understanding of mental illness, his writings to those who are suffering what we would now consider depression contain theological material that warrants fresh analysis. Particularly in his letter to his student Jerome Weller, as we will see below, Luther suggests that he was personally familiar with the experience of despair. Without engaging in unwarranted diagnosis of Luther's own mental health, we can still recognize his firsthand experience of despair as shaping his account of God's grace and its effect upon those who are suffering and suicidal.

Luther on Suicide

Luther writes explicitly about the causes of suicide and its implications for the Christian's soul in several documents. The first is a letter of condolence written in December 1528 to the widow of a man who took his own life, and he also writes separate letters to a married couple about the husband's despair in November 1532. There is a Table Talk, a summary of a conversation Luther had with a group of interlocutors, recorded by Viet Dietrich in April 1532, regarding suicide, damnation, and transmission of teachings on suicide to ordinary people. In addition, Luther writes a letter in July 1530 to a theology student and member of Luther's household who was also his children's tutor, Jerome Weller, in which Luther describes his own struggle with "melancholy," suggesting a possible basis for the formation of his teaching on suicide. This letter is the basis for the sermon Luther preaches in the film after the fictional suicide of the young man, although the words are positioned in the film perhaps 12 years earlier than the actual date of composition.

The first of Luther's letters is addressed to a Widow Margaret. Her late husband's circumstances are unusual in that he attempted suicide (by means that are not explicit in Luther's letter) but did not die immediately. Before his death the man confessed his faith in Christ and was apparently lucid. Luther does not appear to have known the recipient personally; the letter opens, "Grace and peace in Christ. Honored, virtuous Lady: Your son N has told me of the grief and misfortune that have befallen you in the death of your dear husband, and I am moved by Christian love to write you this letter of consolation."[12] Perhaps Luther's teachings about suicide were known to the son of this family, here referred to only as N, before he approached Luther, seemingly with a request for this letter of consolation to his mother. Perhaps Luther's own position develops as he seeks to comfort the widow in her grief. From the opening lines of the letter, however, it is clear that Luther takes pains to establish his respect for the widow and for her late husband.

The letter continues, "It should comfort you to know that in the hard struggle in which your husband was engaged, Christ finally won the victory. Besides, it should console you to know that when your husband died he was in his right mind and had Christian confidence in our Lord, which I was exceedingly glad to hear. Christ himself struggled like this in the Garden, yet he won the victory at last and was raised from the dead."[13] The two issues—one of Christ's victory in the struggle of the husband and one of the husband's ability to express his faith in God—do not seem causally related to Luther. That is, he does not argue in this letter (and does not argue in his Table Talk) that a person is safe from damnation after attempting suicide if and only if he or she can make a confession of Christian faith prior to death, surely an unusual situation. Although Luther expresses his gladness for this turn of events, in the case of Margaret's husband this act of repentance and confession of faith is not the event on which the man's salvation depends. Rather, this confession of faith seems to reinforce what we will see is Luther's general position—that suicide does not necessarily entail damnation. This exceptional situation, the confession of faith after the act that leads to the death, is evidence to Luther of the soundness of his general rule, and he draws attention to it particularly to console Margaret.

The last line of this paragraph, the reference to Jesus in Gethsemane, is the most rhetorically compelling. Seeking to place the man's suffering in the context of the larger picture of God's interaction with human beings, Luther chooses what is surely the most impressive comparison possible: he suggests that the man's suffering was like the suffering of Christ himself. His reminder of the resurrection of Jesus after his suffering and death suggests that like Jesus, Margaret's late husband will also experience eternal life, a promise explicit in the opening line of the paragraph: Luther holds that Christ is triumphant in the matter of the struggle over this man's soul.

Next, Luther moves to the matter of what happened to cause Margaret's husband to end his life. He writes, "That your husband inflicted injury upon himself may be explained by the devil's power over our members."[14] In his book *Choosing Death: Suicide and Calvinism in Early Modern Geneva*, Jeffery Watt notes that H. C. Erik "Midelfort finds that references to the devil as a cause of mental disorders were rare prior to 1520, becoming much more common thereafter."[15] In offering this explanation, then, Luther is expressing a commonly held point of view about the powers and techniques of the devil; the important difference between Luther's analysis and the common view is that while the work of the devil was widely seen as a cause of suicide in his period, the typical reaction was to regard the person who had ended his or her life as thereby cut off from Christian hopes for salvation.[16] Contrary to this line of argument, Luther continues in his letter to Margaret, "[The devil] may have directed your husband's hand, even against his will. For if your husband had done what he did of his own free will, he would surely not have come to himself and turned to Christ with such a confession of faith."[17] Again, Luther does not argue that it is because of this coming to himself and this confession of faith that Margaret's husband is not damned; he suggests instead that the man's confession of faith demonstrates the larger principle at work. While the devil can gain power over human minds and bodies, this power is not decisive and overwhelming and cannot send a person to hell. Christ prevails, even if the person has already been killed by the interference of the devil. Thus, neither can a person's actions thwart his or her salvation, nor can the devil's actions. God's sovereignty over human salvation remains intact no matter the cause of a person's death. This position is an instance of Luther applying the doctrine of salvation by grace alone; he rejects the inverse of that belief, that human beings could wrest damnation from an otherwise gracious God through their own actions. Thus, even suicide cannot reverse the efficacy of God's salvific grace.

Luther closes his letter to Margaret by offering her appropriate biblical verses to comfort her. He writes, "You ought therefore to be content with God's will and number yourself among those of whom Christ says, 'Blessed are they that mourn; for they shall be comforted.' All the saints have to sing the psalm, 'For thy sake we are killed all the day long; we are counted as sheep for the slaughter.' "[18,19] He concludes, "Thank God, too, for the great blessing of his that your husband did not remain in his despair, as some do, but was lifted out of it by God's grace and in the end had faith in the Word of Christ. Of such it is said, 'Blessed are the dead that die in the Lord' and Christ himself says, in John, ch. 11, 'He that believeth in me, though he were dead, yet shall he live.' God the Father comfort and strengthen you in Christ Jesus. Amen." Although Luther emphasizes again the importance of the dead man's expression of faith after his suicidal actions, it is again clear that it is not a condition of salvation that a person who has ended his or her life be able to offer such a confession. Instead, this confession of faith is rhetorically positioned by Luther as an added comfort to Margaret: she has what many survivors of those who kill themselves do not, assurance of her husband's ongoing faith. Faith does not preclude suicide, Luther argues, and suicide does not preclude salvation.

Luther is equally clear in the Table Talk from 1532 that suicide does not necessarily mean a person is cut off from salvation. As transcribed by Veit Dietrich, Luther says, "I don't share the opinion that suicides are certainly to be damned. My reason is that they do not wish to kill themselves but are overcome by the power of the devil."[20] Thus far, Luther's position reflects what he wrote to the Widow Margaret in 1528. He continues, "However, this ought not be taught to the common people, lest Satan be given an opportunity to cause slaughter, and I recommend that popular custom be strictly adhered to according to which [the body] is not carried over the threshold, etc."[21] This is a pragmatic acknowledgment of both the prevailing beliefs about suicide in Luther's period and Luther's worldview—also dominant in his time—of the power of the devil.

Watt argues, "Virtually all sixteenth-century thinkers, Protestant or Catholic, agreed that regardless of circumstances, suicide was wrong."[22] Midelfort argues that the practice of removing the body through a means other than the primary door is part of a larger tradition of "dishonoring the corpse by hauling out of the house through a hole in the wall or through a window or under the door-sill, in order to make it difficult for the uneasy, vagrant soul to find its way back."[23] He observes, "It may be important that Luther could sympathize with the souls of those whom the devil drove to death, but just as important that he frequently expressed his horror at those who took the easy way out of the troubles of this world."[24] Luther clearly does not think suicide is a good idea, but he does see the event as having a purpose, and—however perplexingly—enacted ultimately by God.

Luther continues in the Table Talk, "Such persons do not die by free choice or by law, but our Lord God will dispatch them as he executes a person through a robber. Magistrates should treat them quite strictly, although it is not plain that their souls are damned. However, they are examples by which our Lord God wishes to show that the devil is powerful and also that we should be diligent in prayer. But for these examples, we would not fear God. Hence he must teach us in this way."[25] Luther has a threefold argument here: One, the person who kills himself or herself is not acting according to his or her own wishes; the devil's power is at work. Thus, second, a person who is so tormented by the devil cannot be assumed to have surrendered his or her salvation. Third, God permits this to happen; indeed, God is the author of human action in suicide as in other sudden, unexpected deaths such as murder.

This is a complicated argument; as always, Luther affirms the sovereignty and power of God, in this case to control the devil and to make use of a person's death by his or her own hand to instill proper fear of the devil and prompt a turn toward God in those who know the deceased or hear the story. Luther argues that God does this to illustrate the power of sin and cause Christians to pray (presumably both for protection from the devil and to God, out of piety). Thus telling "the common people" that God is dispatching people by means of suicide and via the devil's intervention, as an opportunity for teaching those who are affected and those who are their survivors, and that suicides need not fear hell might prevent proper resistance to the devil's actions and actually endanger more human beings.

This helps explain Luther's affirmation that civil authorities should continue to treat suicide as a crime, which would have included confiscating the person's property rather than permitting the family to inherit.[26] Luther is weighing the relative merits of affirming the sovereignty of God against comforting the ordinary person affected by suicide, and decisively favors the former. This is, as always for Luther, good news: God alone holds the power of granting salvation. Yet despite the injunction against teaching this belief widely, his position on suicide does not seem to be a secret, merely a doctrine that should not be promulgated lest it have unintended consequences. He is also consistent in rejecting the idea that a person who dies by suicide is forfeiting salvation.

What of the possibility of resisting the devil's power? Three of Luther's letters of consolation regarding suicide or despair suggest he thinks ordinary human beings can to some degree hold off the devil when he attempts to cause them to fall into despair. In November 1932, some eight months after the Table Talk, Luther writes a letter both to a man who has apparently expressed to his family some suicidal ideation and to the man's wife. Luther's letter to Jonas von Stockhausen, the husband, reads:

> Good friends have informed me that the evil one is tempting you severely with weariness of life and longing for death. My dear friend, it is high time that you cease relying on and pursuing your own thoughts. Listen to other people who are not subject to this temptation. Give the closest attention to what we say, and let our words penetrate your hearts.... Since you must be certain and must understand that God gives you life and does not now desire your death, your thoughts should yield to this divine will.[27]

While Luther has argued only recently, in the Table Talk, that God's will is enacted when people commit suicide, here he counsels von Stockhausen to look to Christ, who overcame despair and followed God's will. He writes, "Our Lord Christ also found life to be unpleasant and burdensome, yet he was unwilling to die unless it was his Father's will. He fled from death, held onto life as long as he could, and said, 'My time is not yet come.'"[28] This reference to Jesus's suffering and death does not follow the same lines as Luther's letter to Widow Margaret, perhaps to avoid encouraging von Stockhausen to pursue suicide. Instead, Luther counsels resistance. Luther cites Elijah, Jonah, and "other prophets" as similar models: "[T]hey had to fight against their weariness of life and continue to live until their hour had come."[29] So just as in the letter to the Widow Margaret, Luther compares the man suffering from despair to Christ himself; however, here he argues that it is in resisting melancholy that the ordinary person must imitate Christ.

Luther offers a dialogue for von Stockhausen to repeat to himself: "Accordingly you must be resolute, bid yourself defiance, and say to yourself wrathfully, 'Not so, good fellow. No matter how unwilling you are to live, you are going to live and like it! This is what God wants, and this is what I want too. Begone, you thoughts of the devil! To hell with dying and death! You will get nowhere with me!'" What is to be most avoided, Luther suggests, is to give in to the melancholy thoughts without resistance. Luther offers several other potential retorts to the devil, including dismissing the troubling thoughts in favor of eating and drinking, and if necessary speaking "coarsely and disrespectfully" and saying, "Dear devil, if you can't do better than that, kiss my toe.... I have no time for you now."[30] He promises to pray for von Stockhausen, and offers hope that Jesus will "keep his victory and triumph over the devil in your heart."[31]

The same day, Luther writes to Mrs. von Stockhausen, and offers her both a blessing and pragmatic advice regarding her response to her husband's melancholy. He suggests light topics of conversation, saying, "There is no harm in your reading or telling him stories, news, and curiosities, even if some of them are idle talk and gossip or fables about Turks, Tartars and the like, as long as they excite him to laugher and jesting."[32] Luther is also plain in his advice about which precautions the household should take with von Stockhausen, writing, "Be very careful not to leave your husband alone for a single moment, and leave nothing lying about with which he might harm himself. Solitude is poison to him.... Whatever you do, do not leave him alone, and be sure that his surroundings are not so quiet that he sings into his own thoughts."[33] While the letter to the melancholy man emphasizes the work of the devil and the importance of defying the devil in favor of adopting other, more constructive lines of thinking, the instructions to his wife are primarily pragmatic; Luther has a clear sense of how external distractions might reinforce von Stockhausen's internal dismissal of the morbid thoughts that seem to be preoccupying him.

Perhaps Luther's double-barreled approach, offering both practical and spiritual advice, reflects his own experiences. He writes in July 1530 to Jerome Weller, a member of his household, one of his students, and the tutor of Luther's own children, about Weller's struggle with depression. Luther's letter to Weller is much longer than his letter to the Widow Margaret or to either of the von Stockhausens. He writes instructing Weller to believe that the "temptation" to melancholy was "of the devil, who vexes you so because you believe in Christ."[34] Here again Luther argues that melancholy and thoughts of suicide are the result of the devil's work. He writes, "You say that the temptation is heavier than you can bear, and that you fear that it will so break and beat you down as to drive you to despair and blasphemy."[35] Whether Weller is actively suicidal is not clear from the letter Luther sends him, but it is evident that he has expressed concern about the rightness of his thoughts, and sees his melancholy as leading him away from God. Luther counsels, "In this sort of temptation and struggle, contempt is the best and easiest method of winning over the devil. Laugh your adversary to scorn and ask who it is with whom you are talking. By all means flee solitude, for the devil watches and lies in wait for you most of all when you are alone.... Therefore, Jerome, joke and play games with my wife and others. In this way you will drive out your diabolical thoughts and take courage."[36]

As he has not with either Widow Margaret or the von Stockhausens, Luther offers Weller an autobiographical testimony, apparently not for the first time, reminding him and revealing to the modern reader Luther's own experience in such matters. He writes, "Let me remind you of what happened to me when I was about your age. When I first entered the monastery it came to pass that I was sad and downcast, nor could I lay aside my melancholy. On this account I made confession and took counsel with Dr. Staupitz (a man I gladly remember) and opened to him what horrible and terrible thoughts I had."[37] While Luther does not reveal in this letter the extent or nature of these "horrible and terrible" thoughts, it seems possible that he himself experienced thoughts of suicide. He continues, "Then said he, 'Don't you know, Martin, that this temptation is useful and necessary to you? God does not exercise you thus without reason. You will see that he intends to use you as his servant to accomplish great things.' "[38] Luther's own reading of his history, then, suggests that he holds this past experience of despair as God's preparation for the work Luther was to do in the Reformation. Staupitz's response to Luther, which does not seem to have involved shock, punishment, or dismay, but instead gentleness and useful religious counsel, was so important to Luther that it is Staupitz whom he recalls when responding to his own despairing student.

Luther continues, encouraging Weller to take care of himself physically and socially as well as spiritually. He writes, "Accordingly if the devil should say, do not drink, you should reply to him, 'On this very account, because you forbid it, I shall drink, and what is more, I shall drink a generous amount.' "[39] Luther gives Weller advice similar to the instructions he gave to the von Stockhausens, encouraging "mocking the devil" and emphasizing the importance of an attitude of defiance over and against a strict attention to moral rules. Finally, Luther writes (using the language that Till incorporated to good effect into the film), "When the devil throws our sins up to us and declares that we deserve death and hell, we ought to speak thus: 'I admit that I deserve death and hell. What of it? Does this mean that I shall be sentenced to eternal damnation? By no means. For I know One who suffered and made satisfaction on my behalf. His name is Jesus Christ, the Son of God. Where he is, there I shall be also.' "[40] This conclusion is theologically crucial for understanding Luther's position on suicide. He is here reiterating his central position that human beings are simultaneously sinners and justified and that although suicide is certainly wrong and ought to be avoided, its commission is not ultimately different from other sins: Christ, and only Christ, can justify a sinful human being, regardless of the nature of the sin.

It is not surprising that Luther's letter to Weller is longer, more self-disclosive, and more theologically nuanced than his other letters, since Weller was his student. The importance of resisting suicide (and any other melancholy tendency initiated by the devil) is to preserve the life of the suffering human being; should a person end his or her own life; however, the power of the devil is overcome by the power of Christ. Thus, it is out of love and obedience to God that a person should resist the devil when melancholy, and mock him, rather than doing so out of fear of damnation.

However vivid Luther's words are, his description of struggle with the devil may not resonate today, and may be deeply disturbing as an explanation of mental illness. Possession by the devil, even possession that can be mitigated by Christ, is not, to the modern ear, much of an improvement over the narrative of the person who has committed suicide and deserves to be damned. In addition to reinforcing stigma against mental illness, Luther's analysis suggests that mental illness might be an instance of sin rather than a medical problem. Although perhaps the language of the demonic can be preserved, it must be redirected to the belief that God's grace is insufficient in cases of dementia and suicide. However, this argument must be carefully made in order to avoid reiterating any connection between sin and disability or mental illness.[41]

Swinton, Dementia, and Rereading Luther

Reading Luther in concert with John Swinton, whose work has the advantage of being informed by medicine as well as theology, provides fresh interpretive possibilities. Swinton, an Episcopalian and professor of theology and pastoral care at the University of Auberdeen in Scotland, is a trained healthcare professional and former hospital chaplain.[42] Like Luther, Swinton argues that the experiences of the body cannot overpower the love of God. However, he engages in this argument using language and imagery that is likely to be easier for the modern person to relate to. Where Luther speaks of the power of the devil over limbs and mind, Swinton argues firmly, "Dementia is not a visitation from a malignant god. It is brain damage."[43] This opens up the possibility of reworking some of Luther's metaphorical explanations of despair, while retaining the important teaching that the failings of the human body are no match for the salvific power of God.

Most crucial for the task of utilizing Luther's teaching on suicide without affirming his language of demonic possession is the critique Swinton offers of Christian theology as unnecessarily exclusionary of people with disabilities. His argument is the result of scientific information not available to Luther, but his strategies otherwise strongly resemble Luther's approach. Swinton identifies the problem of providing pastoral care to people with dementia and their families as a complicated one, in part because of the typically ableist character of the Christian theological tradition. He argues, "A good deal of theology ... hinges on the assumption that the theologian is addressing an individuated, experienced, cognitively able self, perceived as a reasoning, thinking, independent, decision-making entity."[44] With this observation, Swinton identifies a deeply rooted problem, an assumption that the Christian tradition, including its promises of salvation, is aimed at those who are cognitively typical and able to engage in a meaningful, intentional practice of Christianity. Who is excluded by such a de facto assumption? Certainly, this practice does not meet the needs of the people whom Swinton is concerned with, those experiencing dementia. In addition, people with mental illness—whose decision-making capacities may be permanently or temporarily impaired by illness or other cognitive impairments—are set up to be regarded as having deliberately and rationally chosen acts like suicide. Both suicidal ideation and the loss of memory may cause people to slip through the cracks of the Christian tradition. This is a situation that is profoundly anti-Lutheran, as it functionally diminishes the sovereignty of God and tips the tradition back toward human capabilities, including good mental health, as a requirement for salvation.

Swinton's theological response is to provide another narrative for understanding human beings who are cognitively impaired. This is akin to Luther's approach in his Table Talk, where he compares a person who takes his life with a person attacked by a robber in the woods. Swinton writes,

> [I]t is the Christian story which offers real possibilities in terms of the development of transformative counter-stories. When spoken into the experience of dementia, the Christian story has the possibility to reveal and reframe dementia in vital ways.... The counter-story of God does the work of repairing broken or misleading narratives and as such will become a place of rupture, resistance, and change.[45]

The prevailing narrative for people with dementia, interestingly, is not so far from the medieval narrative for people who have killed themselves: the person's identity as a human being and his or her very salvation is thought to be at stake.

Swinton relates the story of a student who came to him, concerned that her grandmother's deepening memory loss was jeopardizing her soul: the young woman said, "My grandmother can't remember Jesus anymore.... Is God punishing her for something? Is that it? Is she going to hell?"[46] The language of demonic possession is surprisingly robust in analyses of dementia as well. Swinton writes, "Last week I had a conversation with a friend who is a psychologist and committed Christian. When I mentioned that I was developing a theology of dementia, her response was quite calm, but stark: 'Is there such a thing as a theology of dementia? Is it not just demonic?' I nearly fell off my chair! My friend seemed to believe that dementia was a visitation from an evil spirit rather than a natural biological phenomenon."[47] Although neither speaker was presuming to establish Christian doctrine, both situations reveal that in the faith of the average Christian, cognitive or mental capacity may be strongly tied to the possibility of salvation, and the presence of the devil may still be used as an explanation for human illness.

In an effort to rewrite the Christian theological response to dementia and other experiences of loss of physical and intellectual capacity, Swinton focuses on Jesus's own feelings of abandonment as he quotes Psalm 22 from the cross: "My God, my God, why have you forsaken me?"[48] His emphasis on the divine compassion embodied in Jesus's incarnate suffering and resurrection puts him in company with Luther, establishing significant similarities between their approaches to pastoral care. Swinton writes, "In the passion and affliction of Jesus, we can see pain, loss, abandonment, and deep lament, which in a very real sense mirrors the experience of dementia for carer and cared for.... And yet in and through the pain and affliction of Jesus, we encounter redemption."[49] The shift here is from the capabilities of the person with dementia to express a Christian identity or affirm Christian faith to the capability of God to be present in love and compassion alongside any suffering human being.

On a practical level, Swinton advises increased participation by the church in supporting people with dementia. He suggests, arguing from medical studies of people with dementia, that the lifelong experiences of people with dementia may be rediscovered and revived even as memory fails, especially through return to familiar routines and to worship settings and religious music. Similarly, Luther's ongoing exhortations to his readers, whether their problem is loss of a family member, anxiety, or despair, is that they return to Scripture and to the promise of salvation in Christ.

Swinton emphasizes that the bodily experience of dementia must be distinguished from the spiritual experience of being loved by God. What Swinton provides for modern readers of Luther is, then, twofold. First is an explicit critique and rejection of longstanding Christian presumptions of able-bodiedness and intellectual capability. This affirms the core of Luther's teaching about suicide: it does not disqualify a person from salvation; even those experiencing severe mental illness are part of the body of Christ.

Second is a framework for understanding Luther's now-problematic reliance on the devil as a counternarrative that retells the story of the person who has committed or attempted suicide. What is Luther doing here? Swinton walks us through the process. The human being, in Swinton's reading, remains himself or herself, a beloved and valuable child of God, eligible for salvation and the subject of God's love and knowledge regardless of cognitive capacity. Dementia cannot remove a person from the sphere of God's love. Similarly, Luther's metaphor of demonic possession mitigates the responsibility of a person who is suicidal for the destructive act of suicide. By explicitly naming the devil as the responsible party in the suicide—and by establishing the devil's status as subject to God's power—Luther removes moral culpability from the individual person who has committed suicide. He gives us vivid language with which to describe the idea that loss of cognition or mental illness could lead to damnation. On Luther's reading, suicide cannot cancel out the power of God's salvific love.[50]

Although Luther wrote well before the modern understanding of mental illness developed, his letters of consolation offer potential for modern people struggling with problems of body and spirit. Swinton's work on dementia provides a framework with which to reread Luther's letters and develop them into a robust and modern Lutheran pastoral care response to persons experiencing depression and despair.

CHAPTER FOUR

Feminism, Reproductive Rights, and Disability: Conflicting Accounts of Autonomy

Introduction

In writer Emily Rapp's frank and fascinating 2013 memoir, *The Still Point of the Turning World*, and a number of related articles, she tells the story of her son Ronan. He was born with Tay-Sachs, a fatal genetic disorder that slowly reverses an infant's intellectual and physical development. He died from the disease in February 2013, shortly before his third birthday. Rapp recounts that although she was tested for Tay-Sachs when pregnant, Ronan's condition was undiagnosed. Writing in *Slate* in 2012, Rapp is heartbreakingly blunt:

> If I had known Ronan had Tay-Sachs ... I would have found out what the disease meant for my then unborn child; I would have talked to parents who are raising (and burying) children with this disease, and then I would have had an abortion. Without question and without regret, although this would have been a different kind of loss to mourn and would by no means have been a cavalier or uncomplicated, heartless decision. I'm so grateful that Ronan is my child. I also wish he'd never been born; no person should suffer in this way—daily seizures, blindness, lack of movement, inability to swallow, a devastated brain—with no hope for a cure. Both of these statements are categorically true; neither one is mutually exclusive.[1]

Rapp's perspective is also informed by her own experience of disability. Her first book, *Poster Child*, published in 2007, tells the story of her childhood and young adulthood growing up in Nebraska as the daughter of a

Lutheran pastor. Shortly after she was born in 1974, her doctor noticed that one of her legs was shorter than the other. What this meant was unclear at first, except that newborn Emily had a birth defect. Rapp writes, "When Mom finally told Dad and Grandma the truth about me, that they were still trying to determine what the next few days would bring, Grandma burst into tears. 'It's my fault,' she said."[2] Rapp's grandmother had given birth to her father out of wedlock and had been taught as a child, per her community's reading of Exodus 20:5–6, that the punishment for premarital sex would be that her offspring would suffer: "I the Lord your God am a jealous God, punishing children for the iniquity of parents, to the third and the fourth generation of those who reject me, but showing steadfast love to the thousandth generation of those who love me and keep my commandments." Rapp's grandmother believed that the disability of her new granddaughter was her punishment from God.

Rapp writes, "She was hysterical. She took the blame for me, for what I was: deformed.... Here I was, a condemnation of her life, when all of her life she had been searching for the status and respectability that being a grandmother might restore."[3] Rapp was eventually diagnosed with proximal focal femoral deficiency, commonly abbreviated as PFFD, which she describes as "a congenital bone-and-tissue disorder that caused my left femur to develop abnormally in the womb and left it irrevocably damaged."[4] Rapp's leg was amputated when she was in grade school, and she has used a prosthetic limb since then. Her family was supportive of her, rejecting from the first the suggestion that there was something at odds between being a religious family and having a child with a disability (which came from a member of the hospital staff before they even took Emily home). Rapp's mother told her later, "I wanted to smack that nurse for her messed-up theology."[5] Although Rapp's parents were told she might be intellectually disabled, they rejected the suggestion that she be institutionalized and the idea that her body might represent divine punishment.

Rapp's story is a real, multifaceted example of a set of often clashing religious and cultural responses to disability. As we saw in Chapter 2 and will continue to see, the conflation of disability with moral corruption and sin is all too common in the Christian tradition. This belief, that disability is caused by, is evidence of, or is punishment for sin, has helped support the longstanding and troubling practices of institutionalizing and sterilizing people with disabilities in the United States. In this chapter we will examine that history, consider its present-day applications including the prevalent practice of termination of pregnancies where disability has been diagnosed, and explore the possibility of religious reframing of cultural norms around disability and autonomy.

Rapp's assessment of her own life and her child's life is that, despite her firsthand experience as a person with a disability living a flourishing and full life, her son's suffering was so great that termination would have been not only a wise and compassionate choice, but an obvious one. Rapp was educated at St. Olaf College and Harvard University, was a Fulbright Scholar, and now teaches at the University of California Riverside Palm Desert Center.[6] Since Ronan's death she has divorced and remarried, and is now the mother of a healthy daughter.[7] What makes Rapp's particular life trajectory so interesting is that for a large portion of the twentieth century, as a woman with a disability, her own right to reproduce—not the right to choose abortion, but the opportunity to remain fertile, to marry, and have children—might easily have been endangered.

Even her own existence, looking back, seems somewhat contingent; she writes:

> Here's another set of truths for the moral and ethical mix: I was born with a physical deformity in the age before the evolution of advanced ultrasound technology that may have detected it. My mom did not have a choice about terminating her pregnancy, although when I was born and she was told that I might be retarded, that I might never walk, and that given these possibilities she might want to consider institutionalizing me, she probably wished she'd had the choice. Regardless of what she may or may not have decided had she been possessed of all the information prior to my birth, regardless of the fact that none of the doctor's warnings had any truth to them, it would have been her choice to make.[8]

Rapp's situation helps to illuminate a set of conflicting accounts of autonomy used, respectively, by persons with disabilities and their advocates, by advocates of reproductive choice in arguing for abortion rights, and to some degree by religious people seeking to understand and support the flourishing people with disabilities. Rapp describes the problematic religious analyses of her own disability, affirms her right as a woman, and as a woman with a disability, to exercise control over her own reproduction; she expresses her love for her son, and although she cared for him tenderly until his death, she simultaneously wished him unborn.

The Convention on the Rights of Persons with Disabilities

Another place where the tensions between religious belief, disability rights, and reproductive rights reveal themselves is in the conversation about a UN treaty entitled "The Convention on the Rights of Persons with

Disabilities." On December 4, 2012, the U.S. Senate voted not to ratify the UN treaty, although it was based on language in the Americans with Disabilities Act of 1990.[9,10] Article 1 lays out the intention of the treaty:

> The purpose of the present Convention is to promote, protect, and ensure the full and equal enjoyment of all human rights and fundamental freedoms by all persons with disabilities, and to promote respect for their inherent dignity. Persons with disabilities include those who have long-term physical, mental, intellectual or sensory impairments which in interaction with various barriers may hinder their full and effective participation in society on an equal basis with others.[11]

The treaty has as of 2015 been signed by 160 nations (including the United States) and ratified by 159 of those nations (not including the United States).[12] Virtually all of the world's industrialized nations, and many developing nations, have both signed and ratified the treaty. The treaty describes the precarious position of persons with disabilities across the globe, and is an agreement to support equal rights for disabled people. Article 10 reads, "Parties reaffirm that every human being has the inherent right to life and shall take all necessary measures to ensure its effective enjoyment by persons with disabilities on an equal basis with others."[13] If the terms of this treaty were implemented, people with disabilities worldwide would benefit.

Why is the United States not heartily in favor of supporting such goals? The answer, somewhat surprisingly, has to do with abortion rights. Conservative Christian groups opposed to abortion—even groups and persons vocally supportive of the well-being of people with disabilities—argued that the treaty's language, which advocates for full reproductive rights of persons with disabilities, was insufficiently pro-life.[14] Thus, political and religious groups that typically understand themselves to support the dignity and autonomy of human beings worked to defeat ratification of the treaty, which affirms the dignity and autonomy of people with disabilities.

However, many religious organizations advocating for the rights of people with disabilities offered statements of support for the treaty. For example, the Interfaith Disability Advocacy Coalition wrote in October 2013 regarding the Convention on the Rights of Persons with Disabilities:

> We firmly support the ratification of the CRPD because it ensures the humane and moral treatment of people with disabilities around the world. The equal treatment of people with disabilities is enshrined in our own Americans with Disabilities Act (ADA), which served as a model for the

Convention. Without laws like the ADA abroad, millions of children and adults with disabilities are denied the enrichment of a family life, community resources, or access to the most basic civil rights. The CRPD supports the full inclusion of people with disabilities in society and promotes their right to live independently and with dignity.[15]

The letter was signed by more than 40 religious organizations, including the Episcopal Church, L'Arche USA, the Islamic Society of North America, the Association of Jewish Family and Children's Agencies, the Lutheran Services in America Disability Network, the American Baptist Churches USA, the Unitarian Universalist Association, the Evangelical Lutheran Church in America, various organizations affiliated with the United Church of Christ, and the Presbyterian Church (USA). Similarly, the National Council on Disability issued a statement about the treaty:

> The CRPD protects against discrimination in the area of health in Article 25, thereby underscoring that persons with disabilities are not to be discriminated against in the context of accessing health care. This also extends to the discriminatory denial of health care or health services on the basis of disability including, but not limited to, denial of food and fluids. Both the text of the CRPD and the drafting history make clear that the CRPD does not in any way address the issue of abortion.[16]

Presidential hopeful and former senator Rick Santorum was an especially vociferous opponent of the treaty, bringing his daughter Belle (who has a genetic disorder known as Trisomy 18) to a press conference in 2012 as a sort of living example of his commitment to issues of disability, and arguing in print that the treaty might subject her to death against the will of her parents (quite against many other readings of the treaty's scope and intent).[17] He wrote, "Who should make the critical health-care decisions for a child with a disability? A well-meaning, but faceless and distant United Nations bureaucrat, or a parent who has known, loved, and cared for the child since before birth?"[18] Santorum remains opposed to the treaty, arguing, "There are many troubling provisions in this treaty. A crucial part uses the same language as the U.N. Convention on the Rights of the Child's 'best interest of the child' standard. It would give the federal government, under U.N. direction, the right to ignore states' laws on the subjects of family law and child welfare and possibly determine what is best for our disabled children."[19]

In the wake of the initial defeat of the treaty's ratification, the antiabortion website Lifenews.com reported,

Bradley Mattes, president of the International Right to Life Federation, stated, "This is a misleading measure in that it does nothing to protect life. It is disguised as a way to 'help' the disabled. Instead it intentionally sacrifices the most vulnerable—the disabled and the unborn—all in the name of population control." He continued, "Many don't realize that this international treaty could potentially supersede future attempts to overturn Roe v. Wade." The pro-life group Eagle Forum was encouraged by the vote on the motion to move ahead with debate—because it shows the pro-life side potentially winning.[20]

From the perspective of many conservatives who oppose abortion, then, the treaty represented not progress for people with disabilities but a wedge, potentially establishing abortion rights more firmly in the United States. They particularly raised the issue of abortions not for women with disabilities but of pregnancies where disability has been diagnosed, demonstrating that disability and reproduction are a socially and religiously complicated pairing.

Buck v. Bell and the History of Eugenics

It has ever been so. An important and shocking part of the history of people with disabilities in the United States, with significance to any discussion of disability, autonomy, and reproduction, is the Supreme Court case *Buck v. Bell*. In 1927, the Supreme Court upheld the law of the state of Virginia permitting the sterilization (without consent and sometimes without even full knowledge) of people who were deemed unfit to reproduce. In language that is very troubling in retrospect, Justice Oliver Wendell Holmes wrote of a young woman named Carrie Buck, a prospect for forced sterilization, and her family, "Three generations of imbeciles are enough."[21] In his book *Three Generations, No Imbeciles*, historian Paul Lombardo argues persuasively that Carrie Buck had been targeted as an ideal case for sterilization by the administrators at the Virginia Colony for the Epileptics and Feebleminded, an institution where people who were alleged to have intellectual disabilities or epilepsy were housed in Virginia in the first third of the twentieth century.[22]

Although Carrie and her sister Doris were sterilized on the grounds that they, their mother Emma, and Carrie's daughter Vivian, were 'imbeciles,' the family was in fact poor, of limited education, and of ordinary intelligence. Carrie's mother was falsely described in court documents as having been the mother of illegitimate children; in fact, she was married when her children were born, and remained married until her husband's death.[23] Carrie herself was pregnant outside of marriage; she maintained until the end of her life that she had been raped and impregnated by the nephew of her foster parents.[24] Carrie's foster mother, Alice Dobbs, arranged to have her institutionalized after her pregnancy and then adopted Carrie's daughter, Vivian, whom Carrie did not see again after they were separated early in Vivian's infancy.[25] The correlation between this trumped-up history of sexual promiscuity and the eventual sterilization of Carrie and her sister without their consent went something like this: Women who were considered "feebleminded," whether they were "morons" or "imbeciles," were regarded as especially prone to moral failure, including promiscuity. This made them prone to produce children who were likely to inherit the traits of low intellect and bad morals, and who were likely to be burdens to the state.

The overlap of religious beliefs about sexual behavior and political and social policies regarding people with disabilities reveals the pernicious and harmful effect of the conflation of sin and disability. As Lombardo argues, "The crusade for sterilization gained traction in Virginia with doctors repeating the national cry for laws to combat the hereditary diseases of alcoholism, syphilis, feeblemindedness, and immorality. Some insisted that 'feebleminded women are notoriously immoral' and filled the almshouses like a 'horde of parasites.'"[26] Support for eugenics was widespread in the United States in this period; people with disabilities were at a marked disadvantage if they were also poor or racial minorities, and women were sterilized in greater numbers than men. Lombardo recounts that apart from explicitly identifying people as "morons," coercion to curtail reproduction was applied to people who received public assistance. Investigations revealed that "federal funds had been used to sterilize between 100,000 and 150,000 low-income people in only a few years. Many were adults, and some were children; some were mentally incompetent."[27] A particularly chilling case was the story of Minnie Lee Relf and Mary Alice Relf, sisters aged 14 and 12. They lived with their parents in Alabama; their father was disabled and their mother unlettered. The family was poor. Mary Alice "was born with a speech impediment and had been diagnosed as mentally retarded; she had no right hand." At a public clinic in the summer of 1972, Mrs. Relf sought to obtain medication (presumably birth control pills) for the children, but instead was persuaded to sign a form, which she could not read, authorizing their sterilization.[28] About a year before Emily Rapp's birth, then, a child with a similarly visible physical disability (although having different intellectual capabilities and of a different social class) was sterilized along with her sister, having been deemed unfit to reproduce. The religious backdrop for this action is unmistakable.

Autonomy and Reproduction

What is the relationship between feminist accounts of autonomy and the issue of reproductive rights? Feminist arguments in favor of abortion rights for women are often framed in terms of women's autonomy and their right to exercise control over their own bodies. Significant to such claims is the acknowledgment that bearing and raising children may interfere with a woman's other goals or obligations and thus ought not be forced upon a woman against her will. Pro-life arguments, on the other hand, typically argue that the unborn child has a right for its life to come to fruition rather than be ended; any claims of the mother to autonomy are typically set aside. Philosopher Rosalind Hursthouse points out that attempts to avoid discussion of gender and autonomy when writing on abortion result in "bizarre" constructs:

> Imagine that you are an alien extraterrestrial anthropologist who does not know that the human race is roughly 50 percent female and 50 percent male, or that our only (natural) form of reproduction involves heterosexual intercourse, viviparous birth, and the female's (and only the female's) being pregnant for nine months, or that females are capable of childbearing from late childhood to middle age, or that childbearing is painful, dangerous, and emotionally involving—do you think you would pick up these facts from the hundreds of articles written on the status of the foetus? I am quite sure you would not.[29]

Hursthouse's critique is that any argument about abortion that neglects the degree to which pregnancy, along with motherhood, may interfere with a woman's de facto self-determination is inadequate.

The shared ground, then, between feminists who argue for reproductive rights for women on the grounds of women's right to autonomy and disability rights activists is the conviction that persons must be granted the right to make decisions about their own bodies and minds, and that this right is nowhere more crucial than for individual people or groups of people whose autonomy is endangered by biological, social, or political forces. Although an antiabortion position may seem at first to be the strategy most supportive of people with disabilities, a commitment to the well-being and autonomy of women, including women with disabilities, makes that position very complicated. However, those who are typically pro-choice may also feel extremely reluctant to endorse policies of increased prenatal testing if the outcome is the slow disappearance of entire classes of human beings because of their disability, which happens to be identifiable in utero.

Bioethicist Adrienne Asch, of Wellesley College, and ethicist Erik Parens, senior research scholar at the Hastings Center, note that "many of those who are uneasy with abortion based on a prenatal finding of a disabling trait are prochoice. And many who generally oppose the right to abortion none-theless approve of abortions performed on a fetus carrying a disabling trait. Virtually all the major work in the disability critique of prenatal testing emerges from those who are also committed to a prochoice, feminist agenda."[30] There is not a great deal of conversation between those who would affirm the right of women, including women with disabilities, over their own bodies and those who would argue against the termination of pregnancies after a diagnosis of fetal disability, although there is clearly some shared con-cern for the dignity and well-being of people with disabilities.

Complicating the conversation is the reality that, as we saw in Chapter 1, the concept of disability is an unstable one, and people with disabilities are a diverse group. For example, Parens and Asch argue people with disabilities have a wide variety of positions regarding abortion. "For example, although many members of the Little People of America would not use prenatal testing to select against a fetus that would be heterozygous for achondroplasia (and who could become a long-lived person with achondroplasia), they might use the test to avoid bearing a child who would be homozygous, because that is a uniformly fatal condition."[31] One place to begin conversation is to sort out the impact of social constructs of disability on the right to self-determination of individual people with disabilities.

Constructs of Disability

Disability rights advocates argue, as we saw in Chapter 1, that people with disabilities are part of a socially, religiously, and civilly marginalized group in the United States and elsewhere, and this situation is morally wrong and ought to be challenged as strongly as possible. Disability theol-ogy frames the origin and the resolution of the problem in religious terms. One place to begin is by considering how the concept of disability functions in the lives of ordinary people. Theologian Nancy Eiesland writes, "Histor-ically, rather than naming ourselves, the disabled have been named by medical and scientific professionals, or by people who denied our full per-sonhood. These professionals considered disabled persons to be less intelli-gent, less capable of making the 'right' decisions, less 'realistic,' less logical, and less self-directed than non-disabled persons."[32]

Like disability rights activists, Asch distinguishes between medical and social models of disability and argues that the latter is significantly more useful in understanding the experiences of people with disabilities. The medical

model compares the impaired body of a person with a disability to a hypo-
thetical "ordinary" or nondisabled body and assumes that "if a disabled person
experiences isolation, powerlessness, unemployment, poverty, or low social
status, these are inevitable consequences of biological limitation."[33] The medical model typically recommends medical intervention—surgery, a prosthetic,
medication—to resolve the problem, and sees the experience of the person
with a disability as bodily rather than due to the circumstances in which the
person lives. She argues, "The alternative paradigm, which views people
with disabilities in social, minority-group terms, examines how societal
arrangements—rules, laws, means of communication, characteristics of buildings and transit systems, the typical 8-hour workday—exclude some people
from participating in school, work, civic, or social life."[34] In other words, if
society and its structures—including, as I argue below, the church—are at
fault rather than the individual biological body of the person with a disability,
there is possibility for dramatic collective change.

Parenting While Disabled

One legacy of *Buck v. Bell* is that when people with disabilities do become
pregnant and have children, they may be regarded as unfit parents. The
National Council on Disability (NCD), in its position paper on parenting
and disability, argues, "People with disabilities face significant barriers to
creating and maintaining families. These obstacles—created by the child
welfare system, the family law system, adoption agencies, assisted reproductive technology providers, and society as a whole—are the result of perceptions concerning the child-rearing abilities of people with disabilities."[35]
The NCD statement quotes Paul Preston, director of the National Center for
Parents with Disabilities at Through the Looking Glass, who says, "Despite
the lack of appropriate resources for most disabled parents and their children as well as persistent negative assumptions about these families, the vast
majority of children of disabled parents have been shown to have typical
development and functioning and often enhanced life perspectives and
skills."[36] He emphasizes that parents with disabilities may parent differently
from able-bodied parents, but there is no reason to assume that a parent
with a disability will parent inadequately. However, this is not the prevailing narrative about parents with disabilities.

The difficulties can begin during pregnancy. Suzanne Smeltzer, professor
and director of the Center for Nursing Research at Villanova University College of Nursing and director for the Health Promotion for Women with
Disabilities Project, argues that healthcare providers should follow the

World Health Organization's model of addressing disability as an issue of health and maximizing a patient's health, rather than seeing disability as a disease.[37] This permits providers to "recognize that women with disabilities are knowledgeable about their disabilities, full partners in decisions making, and the experts in how their bodies respond because they live with their disabilities every day and have experienced disability first hand."[38] Pregnant women with disabilities may be looking forward to parenthood and the expected baby may already be a source of joy; as Smeltzer cautions, "Women with disabilities have reported being offered immediate termination of pregnancy based on the assumption that they do not want to be pregnant or should not be having children."[39] She recommends instead treating women with disabilities just like other pregnant women, and assessing their well-being, plans, and expectations. This approach represents not only a necessary recognition of the personhood of people with disabilities, but a clear instance of common ground for pro-choice and pro-life people.

As Robyn Powell, an attorney with the National Council on Disability, writes in an article whose rhetorical title is "Can Parents Lose Custody Simply Because They Are Disabled?," parents can indeed be regarded by the state and even by family as unfit because of disability. Citing the experience of a Missouri couple who lost custody of their newborn daughter and were permitted only brief visits with her, Powell writes,

> This removal was not based on allegations of abuse, just a fear that the parents would be unable to care for their daughter. Because the couple was presumed unfit, for nearly two months they were permitted to visit their daughter only two to three times a week, for just an hour at a time, with a foster parent monitoring.[40]

The reason for the removal? Both parents are blind. Although, as Powell argues, the rights of parents are protected by the Constitution and children are supposed to be removed only after careful review, "these rules have not been objectively or justly applied to parents with disabilities."[41] This family's story is far from unusual for parents with disabilities. This reveals a social problem that churches and other religious communities are ideally positioned to address: many congregations are positioned to provide religious, social, and material support to families with a parent who has a disability. Rejecting the misguided, stigmatized view of people with disabilities affirmed in *Buck v. Bell* and instead welcoming and supporting families is important, meaningful work that can be shared by people with opposing views on abortion.

Harriet McBryde Johnson and Peter Singer

Other issues remain. Two particularly compelling versions of the American conversation on disability and abortion—thoughtful public discussions regarding the relative value of the lives of people with disabilities—have played out in recent public discourse and help to both clarify some issues and raise questions about others. On a philosophical level, disability rights attorney and activist (and person with a disability) Harriet McBryde Johnson and philosopher Peter Singer discussed what it would mean for her if his theoretical positions influenced social practice. In political news discussed below, the state of North Dakota in 2014 passed legislation restricting the rights of parents to choose abortion on the basis of diagnosed fetal disability. The Eighth Circuit Court of Appeals struck down the law in 2015; the possibility of Supreme Court review remains open.[42] Parents of children with significant disabilities, particularly Down syndrome, weighed in on both sides of this discussion, as we will see below.

McBryde Johnson and Singer met in 2003, and engaged in a set of discussions about disability, after which she wrote an article in the *New York Times* entitled "Unspeakable Conversations." Singer has long argued that from a utilitarian perspective, the lives of people with disabilities may be too financially costly for society to sustain. He did temper his position about the ethics of euthanizing people with disabilities somewhat when his own mother was diagnosed with Alzheimer's, further illustrating the complexity of forming opinions and shaping policy regarding persons with disabilities.[43] McBryde Johnson's account of her interaction with Singer begins with a straightforward and provocative analysis:

> He insists he doesn't want to kill me. He simply thinks it would have been better, all things considered, to have given my parents the option of killing the baby I once was, and to let other parents kill similar babies as they come along and thereby avoid the suffering that comes with lives like mine and satisfy the reasonable preferences of parents for a different kind of child. It has nothing to do with me. I should not feel threatened.[44]

Singer argues that parents ought to be permitted to euthanize infants with disabilities, on the grounds that the infants have not yet formed an intellectual identity and thus cannot offer an opinion about the matter. McBryde Johnson notes that "[h]e also says he believes that it should be lawful under some circumstances to kill, at any age, individuals with cognitive impairments so severe that he doesn't consider them 'persons.' What does it take to be a person? Awareness of your own existence in time. The capacity to harbor preferences as to the future, including the preference for continuing to live."[45] Although Singer's criteria for personhood are not identical with those used to justify the sterilization of so-called imbeciles, he very strongly favors cognitive capabilities that are to some degree developed (thereby excluding infants and many people with intellectual disabilities) in his characterization of what it means to be human. His rationale for permitting infanticide and euthanasia is twofold: people with disabilities suffer and thus their lives are less valuable and legitimate than other lives, and people whose living requires ongoing expensive medical care are a drain on the economy.[46]

However, as McBryde Johnson argues in her *New York Times* essay, Singer is taking the wrong approach. The relevant question is not the one Singer proposes, "How many years of your life would you give to be non-disabled?" but "Are you happy, and if not, why not?" or even the simpler, "Tell me what life is like for you." McBryde Johnson writes that although Singer is gracious to her, completely unfazed by her disability, never condescending, and conscientious about her comfort and interested in her arguments, "Singer has his flaw. It is his unexamined assumption that disabled people are 'worse off,' that we 'suffer,' that we have lesser 'prospects of a happy life.' Because of this all-too-common prejudice, and his rare courage in taking it to its logical conclusion, catastrophe looms."[47] She does not make a case to him in person regarding the worth of her life, but writes in her *New York Times* piece, "I used to try to explain that in fact I enjoy my life, that it's a great sensual pleasure to zoom by power chair on these delicious muggy streets, that I have no more reason to kill myself than most people. But it gets tedious."[48] Singer's misapprehension of the value of McBryde Johnson's life, and the lives of other people with disabilities, is only one instance of a widespread problem.

In refuting Singer's analysis, McBryde Johnson demonstrates that people with disabilities are best positioned to offer insight into their own lives, and are experts in what gives their lives meaning and purpose and in what restricts their opportunities for a fully engaged life. This echoes the position of Suzanne Smeltzer regarding the best approaches to pregnant women with disabilities and, as we will see below, similar arguments made by parents of children with Down syndrome. They argue that when seeking information after a prenatal diagnosis, there is no substitute for the experience of families with a child with Down syndrome. These observations are all in keeping with Nancy Eiesland's argument, which we will examine in more detail in Chapter 6, that people with disabilities should be at the "speaking center" when policy about disability is formed.[49] This position is expressed by disability activists' rallying cry, noted in Chapter 1, "Nothing about us without us."

North Dakota's "Fetal Abnormalities" Law

Issues of reproduction and disability are not, of course, limited to pregnancies among women with disabilities. Nor is public policy on disability
limited to now-outdated eugenics laws. A position significantly different
from Singer's, prohibiting abortions for reasons of disability in the fetus,
was recently made law in the state of North Dakota, and then overturned.
Although as the *New York Times* reports, no women were prosecuted as a
result of the law, the impetus behind the legislation and public conversation around it reveals a great deal about beliefs regarding people with
disabilities.[50]

In sharp contrast to Singer's argument that all disabled infants should be
euthanized if their parents wish, the North Dakota state legislature passed a
bill, signed into law by the governor in 2013, that made "selective" abortion
illegal.[51] People with disabilities and their advocates, and people for and
against abortion rights, weighed in at length. Amy Julia Becker, a Princeton
Theological Seminary graduate and author of numerous books and articles
on religion and disability, argues:

> As the mother of a child with Down syndrome, it is tempting to join this con-
> versation by touting my daughter's merits.... Penny's experience is not the
> same as every child with Down syndrome, and yet plenty of other parents
> could write ... to try to demonstrate their child's value based upon the things
> they can do, the assumptions that their lives overturn. But to argue for my
> daughter's value based upon her abilities is to buy into an impoverished idea
> of humanity. Until we learn how to value every human being based upon
> their identity as children, neighbors, friends, and siblings, as ones who exist
> in reciprocal relationships of love and care with others, we will continue to
> devalue every human being.... [W]hat sets us apart as human beings is the
> capacity for reciprocal relationships of love, no matter our age, intellect, or
> economic worth.[52]

Becker quotes Alison Piepmeier, the director of the women's and gender
studies program at the College of Charleston in South Carolina and the fellow mother of a child with Down syndrome, who argues that the legislation
misses the point and that people with disabilities need more social support
to flourish. Piepmeier writes,

> If North Dakota really does want it to be "a great day for babies in North
> Dakota" ... it should make the state a welcoming place for people with
> disabilities. The state could take the cash reserves it has put aside for legal
> challenges ... and train public schools to be meaningfully inclusive....[53]

It could provide easily accessible medical care and early intervention. The state could develop independent—but supported—housing for adults with intellectual disabilities so that there are not waiting lists years long.[54]

Piepmeier, whose daughter was born in 2008 after prenatal tests revealed she was likely to have Down syndrome, argues that prenatal testing in and of itself does not lead to termination. Instead, she argues, the cause of this phenomenon is a culture that labels people with Down syndrome and other prenatally detectible conditions "defective." She writes, "I was terrified when we learned that Maybelle has Down syndrome, terrified that she would never walk or talk, that I would have to quit my job, that I would not be able to love her. Ultimately, I was terrified that she was, in fact, 'defective,' and that she would not be a whole human being."[55] Her fears, she recounts, were based in "stereotypes" and that what she most needed was information about what it would be like to parent a child with Down syndrome.

The lack of access at that point in her pregnancy to a model for parenting her daughter that regarded her child as a valuable human being, along with the expectation that she would need to provide enormous amounts of per-haps expensive care, made her afraid. Thus, as Singer suggests to Harriet McBryde Johnson, it is the social context in which disability emerges, rather than the disability in and of itself, that causes him to regard people with dis-abilities as less valuable and human than their nondisabled peers. McBryde Johnson writes, "What has [Singer] so convinced that it would be best to allow parents to kill babies with severe disabilities, and not other kids of babies, if no infant is a 'person' with a right to live? I learn it is that both bio-logical and adoptive parents prefer healthy babies. But I have trouble with basing life-and-death decisions on market considerations when the market is structured by prejudice."[56]

There are some models of the kind of care Piepmeier might have ben-efited from; Parens and Asch report that the New England Medical Center is one example of a facility where "women whose fetuses are diagnosed with Down syndrome are routinely scheduled to meet with professionals who spe-cialize in the care of pediatric genetic patients. Pediatric geneticists and many pediatric nurse clinicians understand better than obstetricians how Down syn-drome influences the lives of children and their families."[57] At least one practi-tioner at the center reports that rates of abortions of pregnancies with a Down syndrome fetus are "relatively low" as a result.[58] So while Singer argues that prejudice should prevail and that parents should be permitted to euthanize infants who are seen as imperfect, North Dakotans have sought to restrict abortion of such fetuses but have not necessarily fully addressed the problem of an unwelcoming and discriminatory society that awaits them. Neither position offers what seems to be a more effective solution: connecting families with each other and ensuring necessary medical and social support for families raising a child with a disability. Nor does Singer's solution or North Dakota's legislation successfully uphold the dignity and humanity of women and their children, regardless of disability.

Proposed Solution: Where Religious Communities Can Help

There are a series of conflicts between the goal of autonomy for women, especially with respect to reproduction and parenting, and the goal of autonomy for persons with disabilities, including both women with disabilities who want to continue or to terminate pregnancies, and the fate of unborn children with disabilities who are especially vulnerable to abortion. The complications are real and do not appear to have any easy or philosophically or theologically consistent solution. Well-meaning people disagree at every turn, and the history of reproductive and parenting rights for and of people with disabilities in the United States is disheartening.

What might we make of this mess? What is the call to Christian people here? Each person is shaped by his or her society, and that includes being socialized to understand disability in certain ways. University of California, Davis graduate student D. A. Caeton writes, "We certainly aren't irresistibly inculcated by ideology, but nor are we completely autonomous rational beings. Instead, choice occurs within the cultural constraints that ultimately undermine its free operation and which contour the subject herself."[59] Among the factors shaping a person's attitude toward and beliefs about disability are past experience with a person with a disability.[60] Merely being with people with disabilities is not enough. One study examining the rates of termination of Down syndrome pregnancies found that rates actually increased after passage of the ADA; awareness of disability reinforced, rather than reduced, stigma. The study's authors note that "formal integration did not assure social acceptance."[61] To have a positive effect, the interactions have to offer the nondisabled people a chance to recognize people with disabilities as fellow human beings, with distinct personalities, strengths, and weaknesses, just like anyone else. School and workplace interactions may not be an adequate opportunity for positive construal of people with disabilities by their nondisabled peers. Another important and possibly damaging influence is public rhetoric about disability, including news stories, which frequently depict people with disabilities negatively. There is a lack of cultural space for people with disabilities to be welcomed, respected, and accepted.

Healthcare providers are not ideally positioned to close this gap. Medical practitioners—often seen as experts—frequently offer a problematic account of what it means to have a disability. Asch argues that medical professionals are often poorly equipped to offer a constructive and positive view of the lives of persons with disabilities to parents considering abortion after getting problematic genetic test results during a pregnancy. "Until their own education is revamped, obstetricians, midwives, nurses and genetics professionals cannot properly counsel prospective parents.... [Research has] found that counselors provided far more positive information about Down syndrome and cystic fibrosis to parents already raising children diagnosed with these conditions than they did to prospective parents deciding whether to continue pregnancies in which the fetus had been found to have the condition."[62]

These data about how we form ideas about disability bring us neatly back to Eiesland. She writes,

> The most promising model for addressing this real institutional discrimination and submerged cultural imperialism ... is through a liberatory theology of disability that includes both political action and resymbolization. Emancipatory transformation must include not only an examination of dominant practices and beliefs and the way in which they maintain or challenge structures of stigmatization and marginalization, but also a search for and proclamation of alternative structures and symbols of religious life that can effectively challenge oppressive beliefs and values.[63]

Eiesland offers as her primary symbol a reading of the resurrected Christ as the Disabled God: his wounded body serves as a symbol of the normalcy and centrality of finite, sometimes impaired human beings. Rather than being marginal, persons with disabilities are essential parts of the body of Christ.

A Christian church that recognizes that all human beings are created in the image of God and that God wants justice for people with disabilities could reset our social context for thinking about and experiencing disability. Potentially, this support for the value and dignity of persons with Down syndrome could offer prospective parents support in raising their Down syndrome child. Rather than using religious doctrine to control the bodies of—and thus undermine the autonomy of—women with or without disability, religious doctrine could uphold parenting of and by people with disabilities.

CHAPTER FIVE

Recognizing Voices, Honoring Testimony

Introduction

Participating in religious communities may be complicated for people with disabilities; barriers abound. Biblical interpretation, theological constructs of disability, cultural responses to disability, and logistical challenges all contribute to making congregations inhospitable to people with disabilities and their families. A related issue to consider is the experience of religious leaders who are disabled. One clear avenue to transforming Christian congregations into disability-friendly communities is to support calls to ministry, ordained or lay, of people living with disabilities. Why is this so important for congregational life and for the religious life of people with disabilities?

Deborah Creamer, a theologian and scholar of disability formerly on the faculty of Iliff School of Theology and now director of accreditation and institutional evaluation at the Association of Theological Schools, the accrediting body for many American seminaries and theological schools, argues that for a congregation to examine its own accessibility "suggests new theological possibilities in which disability is not simply a consumer or evaluator of tradition but rather a constructive element that offers new options for theological reflection... . There is much to examine, and much to be gained."[1] Called and theologically trained church leaders do not simply serve as examples for people with disabilities (although they do); they do not simply demonstrate a community's openness to disability and commitment to access (although they may). In Creamer's view, people with disabilities have something theologically distinct to offer Christian communities, something Christians of all abilities would otherwise be without.

This chapter examines the experiences of four people called to ministry and trained at Christian theological schools, and identifies a number of themes that emerge from their respective reflections on Christian practice. Kirk VanGilder, an ordained pastor and professor; Erin Diericx, a New Testament scholar who runs an online ministry; Craig Satterlee, a pastor, bishop, and professor; and Raedorah Stewart, a queer womanist scholar, poet, and artist, are all theologically trained religious leaders who are also living with disability, and their respective analyses of their theological training, ministry experiences, and lives as people with disabilities represent a rich theological resource.

Each of these church leaders offers insight into what the church is and what it could be for people with and without disabilities. They discuss the importance of their formative religious experiences in helping them discern a call to ministry, offer critiques of the notion of healing, speak to the impact of nonaccessible worship and fellowship in contemporary congregations, and suggest reframings of disability as gift, as cultural experience, and as opportunity for insight into the Christian understanding of human beings. Each also emphasizes the importance of autonomy for people with disabilities; the tendency of able-bodied people to underestimate people with disabilities and to fail to recognize their personhood is a common experience. Collectively, they offer insight into what it is like to be a person with a disability living out a call to ministry and a clear picture of how the church, including individual congregations, can better support the leadership of people with disabilities.

One important aspect of shifting from the common goal of "including" people with disabilities in ministry to valuing people with disabilities as full and equal members of the Christian family is recognizing and cultivating their call to ministry. Two interrelated practices reinforce exclusion of people living with disabilities from Christian churches; those practices include minimal training in disability for clergy and the lack of opportunity for people with disabilities to be trained in seminaries and divinity schools. These are mutually reinforcing problems: if people with disabilities who are called to ministry do not have the support to discern, prepare for, and live out that call, and people with or without disability who are training for ministry do not have the opportunity to learn the skills of creating a community that is open to what Creamer calls "the diversity of human embodiment,"[2] then individuals and families with disabilities will not find congregations able to serve them. In that situation, the potential for a person with a disability to have a supportive religious community as he or she responds to a call for ministry will be diminished. The loss is not only to individuals and congregations, but to the Christian tradition as a whole.

Challenges for Doing Ministry with a Disability

What barriers, social and practical, prevent people living with disabilities from pursuing ordained or lay ministry? As Creamer observes, there has been significant progress in recent years. She writes,

> Yet even today, people with disabilities are frequently excluded from religious services by barriers of architecture and attitude. Even when congregations have worked to make their sanctuaries accessible, it is not uncommon to find areas such as the pulpit, altar, choir loft, or youth room that still possess significant barriers. Pastors and worship leaders still perpetuate unrealistic images of people with disabilities as pitiful or inspirational.[3]

Complicating and reinforcing this exclusion, for a congregation without good practices of accessibility or a healthy religious understanding of disability, calling a pastor with a disability might seem like too risky a choice.

Outright prejudice may also interfere with calls to leadership for people living with disability. Albert Herzog argues in his book chapter " 'We Have This Ministry': Ordained Ministers Who Are Physically Disabled" that while most denominations no longer expressly prevent people with disabilities from becoming pastors, "many denominational officials subtly question the practicality of ordained ministry for people with disabilities. They emphasize such issues as the limitations in fulfilling pastoral duties, problems in finding appropriate placement, and congregational acceptance."[4]

As we saw in Chapter 1, just as the social model of disability suggests, the challenges facing people with disabilities as they seek ordination and other ministry opportunities frequently come not from their own bodily experiences but from the lack of acceptance from church leaders and congregations. Two important aspects of change for Christian congregations and individuals are recognizing, supporting, and advocating for religious leadership by people with disabilities and educating all clergy about disability.

The effect that pastors and religious leaders have on congregations' understanding and experience is tremendous. Creamer notes, for instance, that access to theological education has increased because of the Americans with Disabilities Act, which has led to changes in higher education; because this process began nearly a generation ago, this means that current seminary students have been seeing "folks like them in pulpits" for much of their lives.[5] There is a cumulative effect of access for people with disabilities upon Christian congregations, but it is not necessarily swift or automatic.

Given the complex set of logistical and social barriers for people with disabilities who are called to be leaders in their churches, we now must ask:

what is it like to be a person with a disability who is called to lay or ordained ministry? People with disabilities can and do become pastors and practitioners of lay ministries and leaders in theological education. The presence and work of people with disabilities in all levels of religious practice and leadership can be transformative. One central question of this book is how best to change religious practice (personal, congregational, educational, denominational) to create churches that more fully live out the call to be the body of Christ. There are a variety of answers, and religious leadership is one very important factor.

Kirk VanGilder

Kirk VanGilder holds a PhD in practical theology and mission studies from Boston University and is an ordained United Methodist pastor. He earned his Master of Divinity from Iliff School of Theology and a Bachelor of Science in sociology at Ball State University. He is Deaf and has served Deaf congregations in Baltimore and Pasadena, Maryland, and has worked as the campus pastor at Gallaudet University. Currently, he is an assistant professor in the History, Philosophy, Religion, and Sociology Departments at Gallaudet University. His research interests include mission work with Deaf communities in Zimbabwe, Kenya, and Turkey, and he has also done research on the religious background and beliefs of Deaf students at Gallaudet.[6]

VanGilder emphasizes that many Deaf people reject the idea that being Deaf is a disability.[7] Deafness is understood as a culture, and Deaf churches are organized around Deaf cultural norms. He reflects back on his own entrance into Deaf culture, which came during college: "All of this was completely new to me as a young man who had spent most of his life with nothing but the vocabulary of, 'There's something wrong with you. You need a hearing aid.' I began to read books, watch videos, learn American Sign Language (ASL) as a second language of my own, and talk with other Deaf people on the same journey of self-discovery."[8] The political activism of students at Gallaudet University was an important part of the formation of a modern Deaf identity for American Deaf people:

> As we Deaf people began to articulate our own views of the world and our community after the Deaf President Now protest movement, there was recognition that while the larger society viewed deafness as primarily a physical disability in need of being changed or cured, Deaf people have rejected this view. Rather than being disabled, Deaf people who rely on American Sign Language, and identify themselves with the Deaf community, see our difference as being primarily one of language and culture, thus an ethnicity.[9,10]

This identity, shaped by shared language and shared political and social culture, also has religious dimensions. Deaf churches reflect not only accessibility of language for participants but also a religious culture of Deafness. However, many Deaf people do not have access to Deaf churches, and this influences religious practice among Deaf people.

VanGilder argues that religious literacy among Deaf people in the United States is typically assumed to be lower than it is for the hearing population; he says, "There's an assumption that Deaf people have less religious literacy because of our lack of general access to religious education and services."[11] However, VanGilder's preliminary research, using the U.S. Religious Knowledge Survey developed by the Pew Forum on Religion and Public Life, suggests that Deaf people have religious literacy levels fairly close to the general population; he notes that this may be because religious literacy in general is "pretty abysmal."[12] There are a number of reasons that religious participation for Deaf people may be somewhat lower than it is for hearing people.

Sometimes the approach that hearing people take alienates Deaf people from churches, VanGilder argues; "The negative experiences at their worst, [are] things like healing prayer rituals that are forced on someone."[13] This phenomenon—the expectation that able-bodied people not only can but should attempt to "heal" the bodies of people with disabilities—also emerges in the experiences of Erin Diericx, below. The attempts fail on several levels: first, the envisioned "healing" does not take place; second, the person whose body is made the subject of intervention is stigmatized and singled out as in need of alteration; third, the community fails to consider what could be done to alter or heal the church such that people of varying abilities can participate fully.

VanGilder notes that there is also what he calls "light exclusion, such as 'we really can't get you an interpreter' which is often with an unspoken 'and we're really not trying.'"[14] He recalls a United Methodist Student Forum event in 1992,[15] which he attended as a student representative. Among the participants were some French-speaking students from Africa; VanGilder had requested an ASL interpreter and the French-speaking students had requested translators as well. He recalls,

> These requests were addressed by having someone stand up ... and ask, "Does anyone here know sign language or French?" Of course, this resulted in two timid people raising their hands. One who had taken two semesters of French and one who had taken a semester of ASL. Neither of these students could serve as an interpreter.[16]

This experience of "light" exclusion galvanized VanGilder, and although he enjoyed the event, when he returned home he wrote to the United

Methodist General Board of Higher Education and Ministry about the experience: "It was here that I first articulated the idea of being a/part as the odd experience of being simultaneously a part of the church around me and apart from it. Little did I realize, this would be my first foray into the articulation of a vocabulary of Deaf theology."[17] While VanGilder was eventually able to respond to this experience with an affirmation of his identity as a Deaf Christian, the danger of such exclusion is that the person who finds that his request for an interpreter is treated as inconsequential will find himself on the outside of the religious community.

Worship is a case in point. In hearing churches, worship style may be accessible to Deaf people or not, depending on the choices of the worship organizers. VanGilder grew up in a United Methodist congregation, and he and his family were regular churchgoers, but his increasing hearing loss set him apart from the rest of the congregation. Like Craig Satterlee, below, VanGilder was struck by the disconnect between the language of worship and his own experiences. He writes,

> I remember singing the ... hymn ["Praise to the Lord the Almighty"] one Sunday, and when we reached, "all ye who hear, now to His temple draw near," I lost my will to sing that hymn, because a thought came entirely unbidden into my mind. That thought was, "I don't hear right. That invitation to draw near doesn't include me." I may have been a part of that church, but at that moment, I was also kept apart from the congregation that loved me.[18]

The congregation's love for him shaped his religious identity and his vocation, but there was still a distance between himself and the hearing people around him. He reflects back on the experience and other similar moments: "We know [the song lyrics are] metaphorical, but it becomes a constant drumbeat without variation."[19] Other examples of typical hearing worship practices that do not necessarily work for Deaf worshippers—a category that VanGilder describes as in between "light" and "negative" exclusion—include "the language of liturgy that is very very mouth/ear centered."[20] He continues,

> In general, classic Protestant worship ... is very orally focused. The centerpiece of the service is a sermon; hymns are the congregation's way of collective expression. So worship is something done with your neck up, and often in unison that presumes hearing, which is why some contemporary worship trends with visuals work to attract deaf folks. But it is often trumped by the praise songs which are super ... repetitive in their lyrics and rely on creating an "emotional state" through the music looping, which presumes hearing.[21]

VanGilder's analysis of Deaf congregations, and Deaf worship, extends beyond the American religious and social context. During his time as a student at Iliff School of Theology, he took courses at the Claremont School of Theology in California, from Kathy Black,[22] which led in turn to an internship at two Deaf churches in Maryland. Soon VanGilder was engaged in mission work in Kenya, Zimbabwe, Turkey, and Puerto Rico.[23] Of his first trip to Kenya, VanGilder writes,

> On one very long and frustrating day, and while I was teaching Deaf children, I had been literally pushed aside by a hearing woman who had felt herself to be a more appropriate person than I was to communicate with the children. That evening, our team met to debrief one another on the various places we had worked that day. I was physically and emotionally exhausted, and had never before experienced the intensity of marginalization and rejection as a Deaf person as I had that day. As I recounted my experience, I broke down in tears. Not wanting to embarrass myself further by having the Deaf members of the team see their pastor fall apart, I tried to leave the room. Instead, I was encircled by the Deaf members of the team—but no one else—as they embraced me, and prayed together with tears of pain in their own eyes. It was a truly holy moment of grace as God's redemption and liberation bound us together.[24]

Thus, the experience of being marginalized by a hearing person led to a spontaneous affirmation of VanGilder's call to mission work and of his value as a Deaf person and Deaf religious leader.

Significantly, this was a double marginalization: not only did the hearing person decide that a Deaf team member was less capable of engaging in the shared mission work, but she also assumed that the best teacher for Deaf children was a hearing person. The experience led the hearing participants on the mission team to rethink their approach to the work they were doing, and remains a transformative moment in VanGilder's religious formation:

> Looking back, that encircling remains one of the most cherished experiences of my life. Having been baptized as an infant, I don't recall it and although I had spiritually powerful moments in my confirmation and ordination as a minister, being fully encircled and accepted by Deaf people who knew my pain in the midst of my brokenness was a new baptism of its own as I encountered what God was doing among Deaf people around the world.[25]

VanGilder's experience of connection with Deaf people in mission contexts, and his identification of Deafness as shared cultural experience, helps position him to identify opportunities for solidarity and connection among other socially marginalized groups. Like Stewart, below, VanGilder argues for the approach of intersectionality developed by African American feminists, recommending the work of Kimberlé Crenshaw in particular. He writes,

> Among LGBT people, there are people with disabilities. Among people of color there are women, among people with disabilities there are people of color who are LGBT, etc. Instead of trying to champion disability rights as something separate from LGBT rights, we should be working with LGBT movements to say "our issues are your issues too. Have you arranged for an interpreter at your rallies? Are your meeting places wheelchair accessible? Have you considered the compound nature of how LGBT people with disabilities face employment discrimination?" ... As they see their issues as inclusive of our issues, our issues will become theirs as well.[26]

VanGilder's identity as a Christian pastor and an academic was shaped both by disregard and discrimination and by the embrace and solidarity of other Deaf people. The ability to see his Deaf identity as a cultural identity and a strength, and thus to reject the stigma of disability, leads him to argue for affinity between the experiences of people with disabilities and other socially marginalized groups, and to advocate for the autonomy and flourishing not only of other Deaf people but of all other marginalized people.

Erin Diericx

Erin Diericx is a New Testament scholar, educated at the University of Wisconsin-Whitewater and Luther Seminary in St. Paul, Minnesota.[27] She also has cerebral palsy, and uses a wheelchair. She relies on aides to help her with day-to-day tasks, but lives in her own home with three dogs. While at Luther Seminary, her academic work reflected her experience with disability. Her master's thesis focused on the pericope in John 9, where Jesus heals the man born blind. She lives out her call to ministry through the public ministry of her website, God the Healer (http://god-the-healer.com), where she maintains a regular schedule posting devotions and reflections on religious life and disability.

Like all four of the religious leaders profiled in this chapter, Diericx was raised in a religious family, and her mother remembers that when she first began Sunday School, the pastor didn't know how best to teach her; the church lacked facilities and a structure to include her in the children's religious education, which was downstairs. An aide took Diericx to her church, where she attended Sunday School and was confirmed. Diericx remembers how a family donated a recliner, which appeared magically in her classroom each year, so she had a chair she could safely sit in since her family did not have an accessible vehicle to transport her electric wheelchair. The boys in her youth group would lift her electric wheelchair into the bed of a truck so she could go to events.[28] While in college, Diericx was a peer minister for the campus's Lutheran-Episcopal Student Movement. She organized Bible studies, meetings, and events. Diericx looks back on this period as having increased her familiarity with the Bible and deepening her faith.[29]

She remains active in scholarly conferences, a necessity because of her location in Florida; she does not have access to theological libraries and relies on conferences and networking to engage in research.[30] On her website, Diericx describes her ministry, which seeks to reframe the notion of healing:

> When I launched the God the Healer website [in] Advent of 2010, I started with the idea of building a community around healing—a community where individuals could learn what healing meant and how to identify where God the Father was actively healing them. Life history, feelings, and ideas impact how each person understands healing, but the common thread running through all experiences of healing is a fundamental change in how the healed individual comes to relate to the surrounding world.[31]

Diericx is emphatically not promoting the notion that "healing," for her or any other person with a disability, entails the reversal of his or her disability; instead, healing is manifest in the breaking down of boundaries between people and between an individual and God.

Just as Kirk VanGilder describes in recounting the experiences reported by his Deaf students, and Craig Satterlee argues below, the expectations of other people that a person with bodily impairment needs religious intervention in the form of bodily healing is familiar to Diericx. She writes,

> Throughout my whole life, I have been prayed over for healing because I have Cerebral Palsy, which affects my muscle tone and my speech. I use an electric wheelchair to get around. To the naked eye, I appear unhealed: I cannot walk.... I may never be cured to truly walk without assistance, but I have still experienced healing in three key dimensions: physical, psychosocial, and spiritual.[32]

Her understanding of her own body and her own life experiences runs contrary to what a casual observer might assume; Diericx sees herself as already healed. Communicating this understanding of healing, and reflecting on the gospel message from the perspective of a person living with disability, has formed Diericx's calling to ministry.

Diericx's experience at Luther Seminary was a good one, socially, intellectually, and religiously. She remembers that while she received the necessary accommodation for her cerebral palsy, the expectations of academic performance were the same for her as for her classmates. Sometimes Diericx has considered further formal education but recognizes the need to balance her ministry and academic work with what she requires to remain healthy and as independent as possible. She writes,

> I'm a scholar; graduate school taught me how to do it, how to be a Greek student and how to make an argument and how to take one point from somewhere and one point from somewhere else and make it your own. I decided not to do a Ph.D. because of the demands of the program. [If I do complete a PhD] then can I do any more? I could teach, but I really don't want to teach at that level. It's too demanding on my body. I work hard to be able to shower, to get into bed on my own. If I don't go to the gym, I lose that ability, and then I need more help.[33]

Her capacity for assessing and communicating her own needs and limits, and exercising agency over her own body and her vocation, is an important part of Diericx's ability to respond to her call and sustain a healthy everyday life. She continues,

> I recognize my own limitations, and I know I can do just as much with a master's as with a Ph.D. For me, the debate involves balancing my physical, psychosocial, and spiritual needs. Recognizing my need to work out and maintain an active lifestyle helps me to meet the physical demands of an independent scholar—holding a book open and turning pages and the hours spent typing. Everything I do requires an evaluation on my energy level and the [cooperation] of my muscles.[34]

The notion of inclusion of people with disabilities in the greater body of the church is also important to Diericx's work. She frames her analysis of disability in terms of the call by the Holy Spirit to the disciples at Pentecost to form a community that includes all people. Like VanGilder, Diericx reflects on the concept of disability. She writes, "The word disability has a negative connotation, and its definition implies anyone with a disability—let alone someone with multiple diagnoses—cannot live a full, normal life. As an individual who has had her disability since birth, I have had to wrestle with what it means to be someone with cerebral palsy."[35] The stigma of disability, Diericx notes, persists despite the social changes ushered in by the Americans with Disabilities Act. She sees a parallel to this situation of stigma and exclusion in the counterintuitive work of the Holy Spirit in Acts 2. Analyzing Acts 2:9–11, she asks, "How could Italians, Serbians, people from Croatia, Romania, and Greece, Asians, citizens of Egypt, Libya, and Arabia, and people in the Middle East all be speaking about God's deeds? … These people did not go together. They did not socialize with one another. And yet here they are, discussing the good news of Jesus Christ and receiving the Holy Spirit together. How could this be?"[36] Diericx sees the Spirit's work as the work of inclusion: "The Holy Spirit breaks down the language barrier, so people around the world are able to hear and understand the good news of Jesus's crucifixion, death, and resurrection. For the first time, the word of God becomes accessible to all people."[37] In Diericx's analysis, the language barrier of the people gathered to hear the preaching of the disciples at Pentecost—the barrier that the Spirit overcame—is analogous to the social barriers that prevent people from disabilities from fully accessing not only the life of the church but the broader life of the community. As many scholars of religion and disability argue, the problem of participation of people with disabilities in the life of the church is not a problem of their bodies or their abilities. Diericx continues,

> In the disabled culture, the day of Pentecost gives people hope that God recognizes many different abilities.… . The Holy Spirit gives people … of all abilities the power to live fulfilling lives to God's glory. The Holy Spirit becomes an advocate for people with disabilities by empowering them with other gifts. People with physical disabilities are able to help the aging population with adaptation to homes and in public, because they understand what it means to feel isolated by barriers. People with cognitive disabilities see the world differently, and they are able to better relate to children since they think on their level.[38]

Similar to VanGilder in his description of Deaf religious culture, Diericx makes a powerful argument that disability can be experienced as a gift. What is necessary is, per the instructions of the Spirit, for disability to be seen as a gift of perspective and calling rather than a barrier. Her observation that people with lifelong experience with disabilities are well positioned to advocate for others is especially apt for congregational life. If a church is set up to accommodate the needs of people with disabilities, then both aging and young members will also find the building and the services more accessible.

Furthermore, this is not simply a matter of kindness or generosity, nor is it disinterested social justice work; when a church community can recognize and support the call to ministry of a person with a disability, the church itself is witnessing the gospel. However, this cannot happen without structural changes, including architectural changes, to churches. Access to the congregation and community has to be in place in order for the gifts of all people to be cultivated and to benefit the community.

Diericx argues in an essay entitled "Breaking Down Boundaries— Physical, Psychosocial, and Spiritual" that people with disabilities have the experience of physical boundaries becoming de facto spiritual boundaries. Some of the problem is architecture, and some of it is perception on the part of able-bodied people: "When it comes to spiritual boundaries, people with disabilities have been shut out of the church in the past. Since churches are not required to follow the ADA standards, physical boundaries, such as steps, narrow aisles, and a lack of space open in the worship space, prevent individuals with disabilities from even *entering* a church—let alone becoming a part of the community."[39] But physical spaces are only one issue. As Creamer argues, attitude is also a barrier, including the attitude that people with disabilities are especially sinful or that their disability is a punishment from God.

Diericx also identifies the attitude of able-bodied people as a barrier for people with disabilities. She quotes Nancy Eiesland, who argues that naming exclusion and rejection of people with disabilities as a sin and "taking responsibility for the body practices of the church that segregate and isolate these individuals and groups is the difficult work of making real the possibility of conversion to the disabled God."[40] One of those body practices, says Diericx, is the belief that people with disabilities would be healed if their faith were sufficiently strong. She turns to the Bible for a solution, arguing that the discussion between Peter and Cornelius and the rest of the early Christian community in Acts 10 regarding the ability of Gentiles to experience the Spirit is instructive to modern Christians regarding disability: "Before Jesus came along, Jews and Gentiles did not mix. The Jews built a spiritual boundary between the Gentiles and themselves, because they believed they were superior as God's chosen people. In the same way, people who are not disabled have made themselves superior to individuals with disabilities in the past."[41]

Although Diericx rejects the notion that disability is the result of sin, she does not shy from using strong metaphorical language to describe the effect that her disability can have on her. In an essay called "Cerebral Palsy Is a Blessing," she writes,

Peace be with you, Cerebral Palsy! For almost thirty-two years, we have co-existed in the same body. You came into my physical body as an infliction from the devil—an attempt to steal my soul from God the Father. However, the Lord has used us to bring him glory. The devil's attempt to make it difficult for me to move and speak clearly has only caused me to do things differently.[42]

This echoes the analysis Jesus provides his disciples in John 9:3 when they ask whose sin, the blind man's or his parents', caused him to be born blind. "Jesus answered, 'Neither this man nor his parents sinned; he was born blind so that God's works might be revealed in him.'" Cerebral palsy, writes Diericx, makes it difficult for some people to understand her speech, "yet the Lord has given me the gift of the written word."[43] Cerebral palsy has impaired her movement, "yet the Lord has blessed me with an electric wheelchair, adoptive technology, an accessible home, and supporting friends and family. The Lord still calls me to do his work, and through our suffering and blessings we are able to demonstrate his glory in the world."[44] She reminds the reader that she is not reducible to her bodily experiences, and it is in the response to and transformation of those experiences that she feels the power and healing of God. She writes,

My ability to name the frustrations, needs, and joys of people with physical disabilities becomes a weapon against the devil, which I would not have without you, cerebral palsy. Therefore, you, cerebral palsy, are a pun between the Lord and the devil. When others choose to view you as a curse, I view and use you as a blessing. Without you, cerebral palsy, I would not have been led down this path, at least not right away, as an advocate and a New Testament scholar.[45]

Diericx is not sentimentalizing her experiences or glossing over the difficult physical or social experiences she has had as a result of her disability, but she recognizes her own agency and the grace of God as more powerful than the limits she encounters. Her call to ministry is lived out not in spite of, but with and through, her experiences as a person with a disability.

Craig Satterlee

Craig Satterlee is an ordained pastor, professor of homiletics, and the bishop of the North/West Lower Michigan Synod of the Evangelical Lutheran Church in America. He is an adjunct faculty member of the Lutheran School of Theology at Chicago, where he taught full-time for 13 years, and at the Lutheran Theological Seminary at Gettysburg. Satterlee earned a bachelor's degree in political science at the University of Michigan, a Master of Divinity and a Master of Sacred Theology in pastoral care at Trinity Seminary, and a master's degree and his PhD in homiletics and liturgical history at Notre Dame University.[46] Although his primary academic interest is in preaching, as a person living with a disability, Satterlee also employs a hermeneutic of disability and writes frankly about his experiences as a blind person with a call to ministry.

Like VanGilder, Diericx, and Stewart, Satterlee was raised in the church and found that his early religious experiences helped to shape his call to ministry.[47] His family was Lutheran and was active in the church, and like Diericx he was the first child in his Sunday School to be "mainstreamed." His mother communicated with the Sunday School teachers and involved herself in the education of the young people in the congregation in part to help supervise her son's experience in Sunday School.[48] Satterlee remained involved in church activities, and an experience with horseback riding in Luther League that he describes as a crisis for the Luther League leaders remains one of his formative experiences of being blind.[49] He discerned a call to ministry as part of his participation in Eagle Scouts in eighth and nine grades but set that call aside, with plans to be a lawyer. During college Satterlee was told he didn't think like a lawyer; he reflects that his world collapsed. He found that he "needed, not wanted" to pursue ministry and enrolled in Trinity Seminary in Columbus, Ohio.[50] His vision had gotten worse during college and had been corrected by the time he entered seminary; the seminary agreed to support his pursuit of ordination and encouraged him to describe his needs, but made no promises for his success.

After graduation from seminary, finding a full-time call as a pastor proved to be difficult for Satterlee. Because congregations were uncomfortable with the prospect of a pastor who was visually impaired, he waited for an internship and was turned down by three congregations. Interview experiences included skepticism about his ability to provide pastoral care while relying on others for transportation, and one congregation offered him a position paying significantly less than the suggested salary guidelines because, as they explained, they weren't getting "the whole package."[51] However, beginning with a part-time call and eventually moving on to full-time positions, Satterlee was able to serve congregations as a pastor and eventually returned to graduate school to earn a PhD.[52]

Teaching has provided Satterlee with both some models of effective community response to disability and the opportunity to clearly articulate his needs and expectations. Satterlee recalls that while he was finishing his doctoral work and teaching at Notre Dame, he realized that the student culture was responsive to his disability. He became a recognized figure within the theology department, and students communicated with each other about what he needed. Even when he was not using a cane that would signal to those in the building that he was visually impaired, students—even students who had never had Satterlee as an instructor or met him—would recognize him in the halls and clear boxes and other obstacles out of his way so he could walk unimpaired. Word of mouth and a longstanding Catholic culture emphasizing social justice combined to produce an environment where Satterlee's ability to walk in the halls was prioritized.[53]

In other contexts, Satterlee has found it necessary to provide explicit guidelines to colleagues and the community regarding his disability. In a document called "Indeed, Bishop Satterlee Is Legally Blind," he writes,

> I assume that, for some, a bishop (teacher, scholar, administrator, ordained minister, someone who has power over you) who also manages a disability is a new experience. Over the years, students and colleagues have found the following "protocol," which I originally developed for the permanent community of the Lutheran School of Theology, helpful. I share it in the hope that it will be helpful to you as well.[54]

The protocol emphasizes throughout one of the most important things any person, whether living with a disability or not, can learn about disability: the individual with a disability has the power and the right to make decisions on his or her own behalf. Satterlee writes, "I am the expert on my vision and how it impacts my life and work. Bring all questions and concerns about my vision to me. Making assumptions and conclusions about my abilities and limitations without consulting me is inappropriate."[55] This observation is generalizable to people with all sorts of disabilities, and is applicable to religious, educational, vocational, personal, and other situations.

Satterlee argues that communities, including religious and educational communities, may not immediately understand the best strategy for providing access for any one individual. Research into best practices is important, but communication is equally important. He writes that "rather than following a set of rules that claim to be universally applicable, the way to begin the conversation is by talking to members and friends of the congregation who live with disabilities."[56] This observation echoes the frustrations of the other church leaders profiled in this chapter, and provides an important model for treatment of not only pastors but members of a congregation as well.

Satterlee also argues that one challenge for Christian religious communities, and individual Christians, is the complex and sometimes oppressive set of teachings on disability found in the Christian tradition. All too frequently, Christians are taught to conflate disability and sin. Satterlee argues, "Based in large part on the language spoken in worship, I would summarize the church's view as the assertion that disabilities are caused by or are a consequence of sin. This view of disabilities is certainly found in sacred scripture, which of course, is the mother tongue of Christian worship."[57] The language of Scripture forms the basis for Christian theology, prayer, and worship, and the belief that disability is sinful, or the result of sin, is deep seated in the beliefs of many Christians.

However, this is a problem that can be addressed. Like VanGilder and Stewart (see below), Satterlee identifies hymns and the worship experience more broadly as opportunities for exclusion or liberation. He relates an experience participating in worship and finding that the hymn "Holy, Holy, Holy" had been partly rewritten to remove an implicit identification of disability with sin. He writes,

> We sing, "Gather us in, the lost and forsaken. Gather us in, the blind and the lame," suggesting that people who cannot see or walk have gone astray and are lacking. Similarly, when God declares, "I, the Lord of wind and flame, I will tend the poor and lame. I will set a feast for them," those who cannot walk are equated with the poor, all of whom will be taken care of, rather than being given the opportunity to take care of themselves.... . With these and many other similar experiences shaping my understanding of Christian worship, I—a Christian who is legally blind—was genuinely surprised when I discovered that the words of "Holy, Holy, Holy" had been changed [from "Through the eye made blind by sin"] to "Through the eye of sinfulness." I found myself pausing to think, "For once we're not judging people who are disabled!"[58]

Instead of unreflectively affirming the notion that disability is a punishment from God, what can and should congregations do? As each of the four people profiled in this chapter emphasizes, one important shift is to recognize that the bodies and minds of people living with disabilities do not need fixing. Satterlee writes, "Many people with disabilities, including me, *enjoy* full and fulfilling lives. For those who will see it, we repudiate the medical model of disability, which views us as sick and in need of a cure, the mechanical model of disability, which views us as broken and in need of repair, and the theological model of disability, which views us as more profound sinners and in greater need of forgiveness than people without disabilities."[59] Once these negative constructs of disability can be identified and repudiated, the opportunity for congregations to be served by, and welcome the gifts of, people with disabilities emerges. Satterlee's connection between the imputation of sin to people with disabilities with the belief that they need to be healed or otherwise repaired is crucial: unwanted attempts to heal people with disabilities stem from the same set of beliefs as do suggestions that sin causes disability, and neither is legitimate Christian practice.

Ideally, the skill of recognizing cultural and religious bias, in whatever form, and rejecting it to more fully live out the call to love one another would transfer easily from one context to another. That is, a congregation or school or family or community skilled in recognizing and working against racism would be welcoming to and affirming of lesbian, gay, bisexual, and transgender (LGBT) people, and people with disabilities, and so on. VanGilder affirms this possibility with his discussion of intersectionality. In some contexts, this process may not be so easy. As Satterlee writes in his protocol,

> I applaud and am deeply committed to our church's mission of bringing the power of the Gospel to bear on issues of diversity related to race, gender, culture, and sexual orientation. At times, I find this limited understanding of diversity painful. I hope and pray for that time when the ELCA naturally counts persons who live with disabilities among the diverse voices that the church is called to struggle with and by which the church is blessed. In the meantime, I need to be disciplined in spending time in communities more attuned to issues of disability so that I will thrive in our church.[60]

Satterlee invokes John S. McClure in calling this kind of conversational practice evidence of a "community of repair."[61] He writes, "In such communities, preaching clears a space for freedom of repair in which persons with disabilities—and all who are marginalized—can speak the truth of their experience and the congregations can receive that truth in the assurance that the response will be forgiveness rather than broken relationship."[62] Thus, talking about disability, and recognizing the autonomy and agency of people with disabilities, improves the functionality and skills of the community, making it healthier.

Another strategy Satterlee recommends for congregations is that people with disabilities ought to be recognized as models of faith in Christian scripture and in Christian life.[63] This is different from regarding people with disabilities as somehow more pure than others or closer to God because of their suffering, or seeing them as an inspiration to those who are able-bodied. That set of interpretations is often dehumanizing and further distances people with disabilities from the center of the community. Nor does Satterlee mean that people who are *healed* are the primary examples of faith; again, this conflates sin with disability. He reminds us, "throughout its history, the church has interpreted scriptural passages, images, and stories that include persons with disabilities in ways that subtly or explicitly reinforce the assertion that physical and developmental disabilities are caused by or are a consequence of sin and may even be God's punishment upon the sinner."[64]

Raedorah Stewart

Raedorah C. Stewart is an ordained minister and trained biblical scholar whose work has included analyses of racism, homophobia, violence, and disability. She approaches disability theology both as a preacher and biblical scholar, and as person with a disability. She describes herself on her blog, UBE: Purple Yam, as "black lesbian womanist poet mother preacher clergy writer painter creator aging differently-abled spiritual being."[65] A graduate of Fuller Theological Seminary and a Passing the Mantle Scholar of the Department of Religion and Civic Engagement at the University of Southern California,[66] Stewart's preaching work was profiled in the book *Weary Thrones and New Songs* by Teresa Fry Brown.[67] Her religious formation has been multidenominational.

Stewart left the Southern Baptist Church of her childhood "because women couldn't preach. Knowing I was called to preach—in spite of being a profuse stutterer and female—by the time I was seven years old, I quit attending my family church in my early teens."[68] Seeking a church home that would both reflect her roots and not "crush ... [her] as a woman, [and n] black, queer" person led her on a long journey. Stewart initially joined a congregation that was aligned both with the American Baptist denomination and with the National Baptists, a black denomination. She eventually moved to the Presbyterian Church (USA) but departed in response to concerns about LGBT issues, and now has dual membership in the PC (USA) and a Baptist congregation that is also aligned with the United Church of Christ.[69]

Stewart's calling as a minister reflects her early religious and social experiences: "I was birthed into ministry I believe from a line of church women who were silenced. I watched the biblical literacy of my grandmother, mother, and aunts relegated to prayer meetings, food service lines, and social activism. None could don the pulpit. The one female great-cousin who founded a church was regarded to be a fanatic and her daughters were ostracized. I knew I belonged to them!"[70] This call to ministry, and specifically to preaching, has been complicated for Stewart not only by social and religious norms of race and gender, but by her own bodily experiences. She writes,

> I was born with a cognitive disability affecting my speech. I later suffered a surgical injury that paralyzed my vocal cords and endured a recreational accident that disengaged neurological normalcy and adversely affected my coordination and mobility.... . While I engage in speech therapy to minimize my stuttering, I seldom bring attention to it. I spend most of my day in silence and I have assumed an unapologetic predilection for typed communication.[71]

This experience along with a long history of social justice activism has led Stewart to formulate a hermeneutic of disability. She observes, "[O]ne is hard-pressed to locate religious or academic intentionality in studying and addressing disabilities in the African-American community."[72] However, the predominantly white academy is no better: Stewart recalls presenting a paper at an American Academy of Religion meeting and discovering that in a venue designed for thousands of people, there was a single wheelchair lift. "The temple of the Academy failed in a most basic assessment of access. It is this measure of oppression that creates an urgency to preach a liberating gospel and seek compliance with the demands of disability justice."[73]

Stewart's initial recognition of injustice within religious communities led her to develop a critique of the church on multiple fronts: "I learned early to resist the racism, sexism, and classism of Southern Baptist tradition, while holding fast to knowing God. Somehow, I know that the church got God wrong; that if what we believed about God [was] true, then how we were treating one another in the name of God was inconsistent."[74] This rejection of racism, sexism, and classism developed into a rejection of homophobia as well. In a sermon entitled "What Is 'the Egypt United Methodist Church?'" delivered on January 16, 2011, to celebrate the work of Martin Luther King Jr. on Beloved Community Sunday, Stewart emphasized the shared experiences of discrimination and exclusion felt by African Americans in American culture and politics and LGBT people in Christian churches.

> It's as if we could now sing "God's Banner over Me Is Love" while waving a rainbow flag. That's the image that comes to mind. It is when we resist defining marriage as being between a man and a women instead of as a covenant ... between consenting, loving, whole adults. The word says, "The sign that you are liberated will cause you to worship me, will cause you to celebrate that I was with you when I sent you to lead my people out, even when polities, and politics seek to oppress them."[75]

Stewart argues here that the problem of injustice spreads throughout the community and is manifest not only in oppression of some members by others but also in the failure of the whole church to worship God. Connecting the theological command to love God and the ethical command to love the neighbor, she preaches that liberation is made manifest in worship of God and recognition of God as the force that liberates all of God's people. Shifting to Paul, Stewart uses his jousting with a Roman official in Acts 22 as a model for how the church ought to function: each person is born a citizen of the family of God. Thus, the sermon demonstrates Stewart's theological position that racial justice and justice for LGBT people are connected.

What do concern for racial justice and rejection of sexism and homophobia have to do with disability? Stewart emphasizes the role of Moses, who is chosen by God despite his apparent unsuitability for the role of liberator:

> I can sympathize with Moses. I can imagine him saying, "But I thought you said you were coming down. Can't you do some God stuff right now? Are you sure you want me, a murderer, to go? Are you sure you want me, a stutterer, to go? Are you sure you want me, a doubter, to go? Are you sure you want me, a poor administrator, to go?" And God says, "I have come down. But you go. And in your imperfection, you have my power to lead my people out of a Pharaoh, out of an Egyptian state of mind."[76]

God's work is liberating work, and God does not reserve the task of accomplishing this work for those who see themselves, or whose culture sees them, as the ideal candidates.

The hermeneutic of liberation, and the understanding of vocation that Stewart has developed, shape and contribute to her analysis of disability, liberation, and preaching. Similar to her recognition that the church does not properly serve and worship God if some of God's children are excluded because of sexual orientation, class, or race, Stewart identifies the exclusion of people with disabilities from the church as a significant social justice issue.

She argues in her article "Made by God, Broken by Life: Developing an African American Hermeneutic for Disability" that disability theology is a liberation theology and that "a disability hermeneutic is ensconced in the tenets of liberation theologies, which have the power to activate social accommodation for the marginalized."[77] Stewart problematizes the popular assumption that what people with disabilities need from the church is prayer for their physical healing. She writes,

> We [differently-abled community members] want Christian communities to feel the tension between dependency and accommodation as the church

wrestles with (or largely ignores) its pastoral duty in relation to persons living with disabilities. Religious institutions often neglect to do more than care for us in ways that are convenient and comfortable, support our families with pity-full prayers and occasional respite, and address suffering and healing as if all we do is suffer and seek healing (on their terms).[78]

Like VanGilder, Diericx, and Satterlee, Stewart rejects the common trope of people with disabilities as people in need of pity and prayers for bodily healing from their religious communities. This approach undermines the personhood and agency of people with disabilities and harms the community by depriving it of capable leaders.

Stewart takes up the story of Mephibosheth in II Samuel 9:1–12 as a text that can be liberating for people with disabilities and uses her interpretation to provide the basis for an African American hermeneutic of disability. Mephibosheth, the son of David's dear friend Jonathon and the grandson of his enemy Saul, had been injured as a child and did not walk well. As Stewart recounts, "When King David had the urge to show kindness for someone in the House of Saul, he offered to restore Mephibosheth's land to him and invited him to always eat at his table."[79] In her reading of the pericope, she first problematizes the notion of healing as a central desire of people with disabilities. Stewart writes, "The text notes the onset of Mephibosheth's disability and concludes with his redemption. The narrative passage *de-emphasizes* his ability and *re-emphasizes* the responsibility of the commonly abled to learn to accommodate the differently abled. It is through Divine intervention that Mephibosheth's honor is restored—honor that had been suppressed by good intentions which had usurped his human rights and political privilege."[80] Instead of healing Mephibosheth's impairment, God causes David to restore his standing in the community and to reconfigure the resources at David's disposal to ensure Mephibosheth's survival and flourishing.

Worship also matters enormously, especially in the constructs of disability it provides. Like VanGilder and Satterlee, Stewart reflects back on the hymns of her religious upbringing:

A church song in the African-American repertoire of gospel favorites is our post-Resurrection Christology which inspires us to sing: "I looked at my hands and my hands looked new / I looked at my feet and they did too." It implies that our intimate identification with the crucified Christ's nail-pierced hands and stake-impaled feet is presented to our new and glorified bodies as unpierced and unbroken. But, what happens to a theology in which Mephibosheth "remained lame in both feet" while sitting at the king's table for the rest of his life?[81]

The restoration of Mephibosheth is social, rather than physical; using him as a biblical model problematizes the conflation of these "new and glorified" bodies with Christ's salvific work. Stewart demonstrates that Christian communities should focus on the liberation and restoration of people to their communities, not on restoration of bodies, which may well be unwanted and unnecessary. She argues that this work must emerge from the experiences of people with disabilities themselves:

> Metaphorical and literal brokenness do not necessarily lead to limitations and exclusions—these forms of brokenness can often be the very agency through which redemption comes for the whole community. I must insist that, while preaching on 'Disability Inclusion Sunday' or considering how to serve disabled parishioners, religious leaders call to the pulpit people who speak from lived experience, without inserting your own able-bodied interpretation.[82]

As we saw above, Creamer argues that disability and the lived experience of disability is "a constructive element that offers new options for theological reflection."[83] Stewart's emphatic position regarding preaching and leadership emphasizes how this option for disability theology can be lived out in congregational life.

Conclusions

What do these called and trained church leaders have to teach us about disability and religious leadership? They envision a church whose physical space is accessible, whose worship language rejects the claim that disability is caused by or is a sign of sin, where the call to serve is not restricted by one's disability, and they emphasize the importance of recognizing and respecting the agency and autonomy of people with disabilities, whether or not they are religious leaders. Moreover, theological education for pastors needs to be accessible and needs to teach a theology of access.

Each of these leaders also provides evidence of a rich, full life and rejects the idea that the church should regard people with disabilities as objects of pity or people who are sick and primarily in need of healing. They provide Christian congregations with a call to reshape congregational practices so that at every point in the life of individual Christians—as infants and small children, as confirmands and young adults, as mature adults with professional identities, families, and households, as elderly people perhaps with growing health concerns—people with disabilities are regarded as legitimate and gifted members of the body of Christ.

Disability in the Contemporary Church: Social Statements and Denominational Practice

Introduction

A recent article in the *Journal of Religion, Disability, and Health* by Melinda Jones Ault, an expert in intellectual disabilities who teaches at the University of Kentucky, included this observation about church by the mother of a young child with a mild intellectual disability: "Our son is often either patronized or treated like an outsider (so were we for that matter). The contradictions were so hard to accept—here is the home of so-called love and acceptance and there seems to be none for people with differing intellectual abilities."[1] This mother's observation—recorded as part of a larger study we will examine later—points to an interesting and problematic dissonance in American Christian theological practice: while churches, including at the denominational level, typically give some voice to the ideal of welcoming and valuing people with disabilities, actual practice can be woefully inadequate, and seminary and other theological education does not necessarily address this problem. As we saw in Chapter 5, people with disabilities can be extraordinary religious leaders, and as we will see in Chapter 7, some Christian communities are successful in creating inclusive congregations and ministries for people with disabilities. But there are still gaps in religious education about disability and religious participation among people with disabilities, gaps that Christian congregations currently do not fully address.

This chapter explores the following questions: What is the current state of theological education for and about people with disabilities? What do contemporary Christian denominations have to say about disability? Are people living with disabilities flourishing in American religious communities? We will take up the critique of one denomination provided by Nancy Eiesland, and assess the progress—if any—of three mainline American denominations with respect to recognition and inclusion of people living with disabilities.

Eiesland's Critique of the American Lutheran Church

Nancy Eiesland, the theologian and sociologist whose groundbreaking 1994 book *The Disabled God* can be considered the beginning point of the modern disability theology movement, includes in that book an analysis of the official statements and actual practices of the American Lutheran Church (ALC), a predecessor body of the Evangelical Lutheran Church in America, or ELCA, in the early 1980s. Although, as Eiesland notes, "No single story about the relationship between persons with disabilities and the Christian church can express our diverse, complex, and enigmatic connection,"[2] her interrogation of the ALC's policy and the connection between its theory and practice is a compelling one. Whether various church policies on disability are theologically robust, and whether those policies match religious practice, remains an open question, not only for churches and not only for issues related to disability. Investigating the connection between what a denomination says about disability, and to whom, and how it and the broad Christian community respond to people living with disabilities is one part of the larger task of disability theology. While measuring the efficacy of theological positions on disability is complicated, identifying the ways in which theory and practice do not match up is an important part of Christian communities' task of self-reflection.

Eiesland observes that the ALC adopted a resolution regarding disability in 1980, in concert with the United Nations' International Year of the Disabled, which was 1981.[3] The subhead of this section of her book, which discusses both the ALC and the United Nations, is "An American Tragedy." In 1980 the ALC offered a resolution on the church's response to people with disabilities and separate statements on education of children and on "Issues and Implications." The denomination's General Convention ratified several related recommendations, encouraging the church to take seriously issues of disability as the resolution identified them.[4] One recommendation that was ratified cites Galatians 3:28 approvingly and argues that the "wholeness of the family of God demands not only compassion for the disabled but also their inclusion as fully committed members of the body of Christ who are able to witness and minister."[5] That is, ordination of people with disabilities is explicitly recognized as a requirement for ALC congregations to be fully living out their identity as a community where people are "one in Christ."[6]

However, just six years later, the ALC proposed a second policy barring people with "significant" disabilities from ordained ministry.[7] Although the policy was never put into place, even its rejection hardly speaks well of the ALC. As the *New York Times* reported, "Herb W. David, a spokesman for the church, said the decision to drop the proposal was more a result of a review by lawyers than public reaction, which he described as 'intense.' The church received hundreds of telephone calls and letters complaining about the policy, Mr. David said."[8] There is a remarkable lack of institutional self-reflection in that candid disclosure by David: the protest of ordinary people on ethical grounds was less compelling to the ALC than concerns about the legality of the policy.

What did this policy propose about clergy with disabilities, and what was the rationale? Ronald Duty, currently the coordinator for Cross-Cultural Conversation at the ELCA, argues that the concerns about the fitness of people with disabilities for ordination arose from two separate issues: there were questions within the ALC about what constituted an effective pastor and whether people with disabilities would be able to meet these expectations. The language of the 1985 document, entitled "Seminary Admission and Certification Criteria in Relation to the Work ALC Pastors Are Expected to Do," is somewhat jarring today:

> The typical parish pastoral role involves conduct of ministry in a variety of physical and geographical settings including the church building proper, homes, hospitals, nursing homes, and miscellaneous community sites.... Thus pastors are expected to be sufficiently able bodied, ambulatory and mobile to carry out their tasks in these diverse settings, and to respond rapidly in the event of emergencies. ... Continuing advances in medical science and technology make it impossible to specifically list all conditions or degrees of severity which categorically will not be in compliance with [established expectations]. However, there are several broad categories or conditions which are potentially disqualifying and any candidates with these conditions require very careful and thorough screening.[9]

The various disqualifying disabilities are identified: "Neurological disorders—for example multiple sclerosis, amyotrophic lateral sclerosis ... longstanding juvenile onset of diabetes, cystic fibrosis, some renal diseases, some non-correctible ... congenital heart diseases ... quadriplegia and some forms of arthritis ... severe psychiatric disorders, especially psychosis and those requiring chronic medication."[10] No clear criteria are provided for identifying which seminarians or pastors with chronic illnesses or disabilities might be perfectly capable of successfully serving congregations, nor is there any suggestion in the resolution that the person with a call to ministry who also has a disability be at the center of such a conversation or that discernment to ministry involve practical problem-solving to identify solutions for possible barriers to ordination for people with disabilities. The recognition in the 1980 resolution that people with disabilities make up a vital part of the body of Christ is absent.

There also seems to have been a perception that people with disabilities were misusing the benefits made available to prospective pastors. Duty writes, "Another concern was raised by apparently a small number of instances in which it is alleged that disabled people enrolled in ALC seminaries simply to have access to the health insurance coverage then afforded to seminary students, but who had no actual sense of call to ordained ministry or no intention to serve."[11] Duty emphasizes that he cannot confirm that these allegations were true or that the concern was widespread, and argues that since the ALC merged with other Lutheran church bodies into the ELCA shortly afterward, the issue was eventually addressed when the ELCA formulated its own policies regarding ordination. Notably, while the 1986 policy may have been motivated by a perception that some people with disabilities were driven by lack of insurance to enroll in seminary, there is no indication that the ALC felt moved to address this problem by means other than prohibiting people with disabilities from ordination.

The proposed exclusion of clergy with disabilities from ALC rosters was not the only failure, Eiesland argues. The original 1980 policy, much more supportive of people with disabilities, did not get traction in the denomination. Eiesland observes, "Despite its broad and well-intentioned goals, the ALC's [early] theology of access was a non-starter. The institutional change it enjoined did not occur; the issues and implications it raised were affirmed as morally and socially laudable but never satisfactorily incorporated into the church's practices."[12] Eiesland speculates about what went wrong: "Although it would be impossible to identify all the factors that contributed to this ironic and tragic twist, consideration must be given to the likelihood that the direction and content of the ALC's 1980 theology of access itself perpetuated the institutional marginalization of people with disabilities and helped set the stage for the denomination's decision to deny entire groups access to ordained ministry."[13] In other words, Eiesland argues that the formation of the policy, while well intentioned, was carried out in such a way as to further marginalize people with disabilities in the ALC.

A summary by Ronald Duty of the proposed 1986 policy on ordination and the backlash against it makes this observation: "Some ALC seminarians with disabilities were certified for ordination and called to parish ministry after the adoption of this policy. It is unknown whether it was ever used either to deny admission to an ALC seminary or to deny certification for ordination during the remainder of the ALC's life."[14] The response of the public that is noted by Herb David, the ALC spokesman, and documented by Duty does suggest that many people both inside and outside the ALC were appalled by the proposal to exclude some people with disabilities from ordination. However, as Eiesland argues, that two competing positions on disability emerged close together from the same denomination reveals that the ALC statement "fails adequately to address the fundamentals of Lutheran theology, that is, ministry, Word and Sacraments."[15]

Where does that ignominy leave us today? In her analysis of the ALC position, Eiesland outlines several crucial features of a denominational statement on disability: First, it should emerge from serious engagement with disability rights activists outside the church. Second, people with disabilities should not only contribute to such a policy, but should be at what Eiesland calls "the speaking center"[16] when the policy is created at an institutional level. Third, she argues that any successful disability statement will identify social structures, not individual bodies, as the problem that needs to be addressed. Fourth, a disability statement should be theologically robust.

Duty notes that the current formulation of the ELCA's social policy on disability and the actual practices of congregations are due largely to just the people Eiesland calls upon, disability rights activists:

> What happens in ELCA congregations is more a function of secular trends in the awareness and treatment of people with disabilities in the larger American society than ELCA policy (since there wasn't a policy document directly addressing the issue until 2011). But, there are small groups of activists on disability issues (comprised primarily of disabled people themselves, family members of disabled people, and some others) who press for practical actions both within particular congregations and by ELCA synods.[17]

Although this is a hopeful sign, there are still other issues to consider. One other problem Eiesland clearly identifies in her critique of the ALC policy statements is the accessibility of theological education to people with disabilities. Where do things stand today?

Theological Education

Ideally, every congregation would be led by a pastor with training in disability and with practice in recognizing and responding to the needs of parishioners with disabilities and their families. Churches would be accessible; worship and other program offerings would be accessible as well. The concerns of disability rights activists about access to the public spaces and social opportunities offered to able-bodied people would also become concerns of the church. People with disabilities would, far from being specifically excluded by denominational policy, be welcomed into seminary education if they had a call to leadership in the church.

One problem facing the church is the current response to disability on the part of seminaries and theological schools. Although things are improving, there is much work still to be done. Naomi Annandale and Erik W. Carter engaged in a study of the approach to disability taken by 118 institutions of graduate education that are currently accredited by the Association of Theological Schools.[18] As the American Theological Society (ATS) guidelines note, "Graduate theological schools equip future religious leaders. The curriculum, however, has usually included limited or no attention to equipping those leaders with knowledge about human experience of disability."[19] Annandale and Carter studied a variety of areas: the schools' curriculum, the perceived challenges to covering disability in the curriculum, students' preparation for ministry to people with disabilities, the institution's need for resources for educating students about disabilities and inclusion of people with disabilities (students, faculty, and staff), and the level of accommodations for disability each school had provided in recent years.

Annandale and Carter found that, "overall, the majority of respondents perceived that their graduates were *not at all* (3.4%) or *only a little* (70.7%) prepared to respond to spiritual and theological questions resulting from disability-related human experiences."[20] Less than half of the schools (42.2 percent) reported that their students were *adequately* or *highly* prepared to include people with disabilities in fellowship at their future congregations, and the numbers decline steadily for other areas of church life: 29.1 percent of schools viewed their students as well prepared to include people with disabilities in the worship practices and rituals of the church, only 25.6 percent said students were prepared to provide religious education to people with disabilities, and fewer still saw their students as equipped to integrate people with disabilities into service opportunities in the congregation (24.8 percent) or in leadership positions in the church (23.9 percent).[21] These data suggest that there is a significant gap between what clergy need to know and the training they are receiving, and between the desire of people with disabilities to participate in and lead Christian congregations and the opportunities for them to do so.

What are the practical implications of these findings? When families or individuals with disabilities become active in a congregation, their clergy are unlikely to have been trained in seminary about incorporating them into the regular life of the community. Annandale and Carter write, "[O]ur findings suggest a focus on people with disabilities often receives relatively limited attention within the theological curriculum. ... Although occasionally addressed in courses addressing pastoral care, religious education, and spiritual formation, disability was less frequently addressed in the disciplines of theology, biblical studies, and historical studies. This represents an important omission in terms of student preparation for ministry."[22]

The results of Annandale and Carter's study suggest two things: first, they found that people with disabilities are underrepresented in schools that provide theological education. This reality contributes to a second important aspect of theological education revealed by the study: schools are not necessarily offering accommodations at a significant rate, perhaps because students needing accommodation have not asked, because they are not enrolling in great numbers, and schools do not typically educate or employ significant numbers of people with disabilities, perhaps because the physical buildings are not accessible, perhaps because the lower rates of enrollment in theological schools of students with disabilities has led to a shortage of qualified faculty with disabilities, and so on. The problems of access and of absence of people with disabilities are mutually reinforcing.

As Annandale and Carter argue, about 20 percent of the general population of the United States are people with disabilities, and about one family in four has a member with a disability.[23] While it is unrealistic to expect that theological schools have a population of people with disabilities mirroring the larger population, there is still a significant gap. "When asked to approximate the percentage of students, faculty, and staff at their schools with disabilities, 4.4 percent said none, 59.6 percent said 1%–5%, 23.7 percent said 6%–10%, 7.9 percent said 11%–15%, and 4.4 percent said more than 15%."[24] That is, only a very few schools have anything like a numerically representative cohort of students, faculty, and staff with disabilities at their institutions.

What are the religious implications of these findings? One important disclaimer: people with disabilities, inside or outside religious communities, do not have any obligation to become advocates for disability rights or educators of their peers. However, the opportunity for all students to engage in meaningful theological reflection with people with disabilities is an important part of gaining a fuller understanding of the created world. Annandale and Carter argue,

Attention to disabilities presents an opportunity to resist cultural addictions to unrealistic qualities such as invulnerability, perfection, and conformity and to find strength and integrity in accepting the reality of human difference, struggle, and sometimes suffering. And disabilities bring to the forefront some of the most critical, eternal questions for faith communities: Will they welcome, affirm, and incorporate, and celebrate all people? How will the larger community care for those with particular vulnerabilities? Will all people be open to receive care as well? Clearly, questions related to disability point at the heart of what it means to be human and to live in human community, including faith communities.[25]

The issues raised by the participation of people with disabilities are not narrow, specific problems that apply only to a few people, but opportunities for every person to consider his or her humanity and relationship to God more fully, and to reflect on the very nature of God. Although the results of Annandale and Carter's study are disheartening in some ways, there have been changes in recent years, and the opportunity for denominations, schools, and individual students to reflect more deeply on the human experience should not be overlooked, for the well-being not only of church members who have disabilities but for the community as a whole. As the policy guidelines for the ATS argue,

God takes special delight in the creation of persons as made in the image of God, each with unique gifts and capabilities. The ministry of Christ demonstrates that divine hospitality is available to all persons and that human barriers designating some as inferior are forever destroyed. The resurrection shows us the power of God to overcome all human attempts at limiting God's love, even death itself. ... If issues of disability are central to understanding both divine care and the character of the church, then certainly issues of disability should play a crucial role in Christian ministerial formation.[26]

The ATS policy statement provides an argument that people with disabilities are made in the image of God and thus ought to be regarded as equal, not inferior, to other human beings. In addition, the experiences of people with disability illuminate the human relationship to God and provide a perspective essential to healthy church communities. Recognition of people living with disabilities as equal members of the Christian family is not only right, but beneficial to all involved.

Denominational Responses

To what extent is this work underway already? It is not an exaggeration to say that Eiesland's book spurred a movement. While many denominations had begun to reflect on and write about disability, and organize accommodations for people with disabilities prior to the publication of *The Disabled God*, that work has blossomed in recent years. The field of disability theology, and its sister field of disability-focused biblical interpretation, is now well established and still growing, but as we have seen throughout this book, significant practical and theological barriers remain for people with disabilities both inside and outside Christian churches. Since Eiesland's book was published, and in no small part because of her work, many Christian denominations have continued to refine their teaching and practices around disability.

We will now take up the statements and resources on disability provided by the Roman Catholic Church and two mainline Protestant denominations, the Presbyterian Church (USA) and the ELCA (which includes the ALC as one of its predecessor bodies).[27] As we will see, terminology to describe people, disability, and religious belief and practice varies widely from one denomination to the next, and the import of an official statement varies from tradition to tradition. The resources that each denomination provides are different but share some common features, and in many cases the materials could easily be adopted by members of another denomination. However, in a general sense, each of the documents we will consider below is a position statement of the denomination, providing guidance but not a strict set of requirements for participating congregations.

Roman Catholic

The current American Roman Catholic statement on disability was first published in 1978 as the *Pastoral Statement of U.S. Catholic Bishops on Handicapped People* and was updated in 1989 to the *Pastoral Statement of U.S. Catholic Bishops on People with Disabilities.* While the language is now more contemporary, the structure and content of the document are otherwise intact. It provides 35 short statements on topics ranging from the affirmation of family members of people with disabilities as a valuable resource in providing ministry,[28] to the condemnation of abortion of fetuses with disabilities,[29] to recommendations at the parish, diocesan, and national levels. There is also a Catholic-specific organization called the National Catholic Partnership on Disability (NCPD), which "was established in 1982 to implement in parishes and dioceses throughout the United States the 1978 *Pastoral Statement of U.S. Catholic Bishops on Persons with Disabilities.*"[30] The NCPD's website offers a range of resources that could be used by Christians of various denominations. In addition to this statement, broader Catholic social teaching, will see in Chapter 7, serves as an important guide for congregations interested in addressing exclusion of people with disabilities from religious and social life.

Presbyterian Church (USA)

The Presbyterian Church (USA), hereafter the PC(USA), also has a long-established theological position on disability, and it provides sophisticated set of resources for its congregations. The original statement on disability from the PC(USA) was passed in 1977 and is called *That All May Enter.*[31] The statement was reaffirmed in 2000 and remains an important guiding document for the denomination. A lengthy guide for congregations called "Living into the Body of Christ: Towards Full Inclusion of People with Disabilities" was approved in 2006,[32] and guides are created each year for Disability Access/Inclusion Sunday.

The PC(USA) is notable as one denomination that includes research on religious participation by families with a child or children with a disability in its *2013 Disability Inclusion Resource Packet*. The resource packet is free and includes a wide variety of documents, including worship resources that could easily be used by non-Presbyterian congregations and numerous short narratives from people with disabilities and people who are leaders and members of congregations with successful disability ministries. The PC(USA) includes in its materials evidence-based arguments about church participation, including an essay by Melinda Jones Ault. The materials are easily accessed and practical, and represent a long-standing practice of work toward inclusion of people with disabilities in the denomination.

Evangelical Lutheran Church in America

The ELCA[33] has also provided a lengthy social message on disability, completed in 2010 (along with a separate social message on mental illness and a social statement on genetics). While social statements are intended to establish ELCA positions, social messages are designed to "address pressing contemporary concerns in light of the prophetic and compassionate traditions of Scripture and do not establish new teaching or policy. Rather, they build upon previously adopted teaching and policy positions, especially from social statements."[34]

Thus, the ELCA message on disability is not supposed to break new ground; rather, it is supposed to elaborate on existing theological positions and ecclesial practices. These include the 1980 ALC statement discussed above, a set of actions taken by the 1989 ELCA Churchwide Assembly, and the work of the Division for Social Ministry Organizations, begun in 1988.[35]

The ELCA has a number of organizations within the denomination designed to support people with disabilities, including the ELCA Disability Mentor Network, the Definitely Abled Advisory Committee, and the Lutheran Network on Mental Illness/Brain Disorders.

Analysis of Denominational Statements

A variety of themes emerge when the various social statements are read alongside each other. To some degree, the problems Eiesland identified in the ALC statement are addressed in each of the three denominational positions described above. Recall that Eiesland had concerns about the theological claims of the ALC statement, the lack of engagement with disability rights activism, the lack of participation by people with disabilities in creating the statement, and the mistaken identification of the bodies of people with disabilities, rather than established social structures, as problematic. (In other words, the church looked just like the world in many ways.)

The theology of the three statements is prominent and clearly grounded in denominational teachings and interpretation of the Bible. Common theological claims across the Roman Catholic, PC(USA), and ELCA positions include a universal affirmation of the *Imago Dei*. The Roman Catholic and Presbyterian documents include some discussion of the significance of Jesus's miracles of healing; the ELCA and PC-USA statements both focus on the Pauline metaphor of the body in I Corinthians 12; the Presbyterian statement repeatedly uses the metaphor of the body of Christ, including in the title of the document, to argue for full inclusion of all people in the life of the church. Both the ELCA and PC(USA) statements invoke Galatians 3:27–28 to argue for a theological basis of inclusion. While the Roman Catholic statement does not invoke Galatians in this way, it does argue for the "common humanity underlying all distinction" and invokes Romans 13:9 and the obligation to love one's neighbor as oneself as biblical support.[36]

The statements also focus critique on the society that fosters discrimination and exclusion of people with disabilities. The Roman Catholic and Presbyterian statements both explicitly affirm justice as a goal of the church for society; the 2000 Presbyterian affirmation of its 1978 statement *That All May Enter* reads in part, "The liberated people of God are called into a covenant that requires justice and righteousness. The people of God understand that we are responsible for treating others the way God treats us."[37] This claim is grounded in Amos 5:24 and Micah 6:8, both of which enjoin the people of God to "work for justice."[38] The ELCA statement identifies the problem as sin: it frames the tendency of human beings to favor an illusory ideal of human independence, at the expense of people with disabilities, as idolatry: "This mindset ... substitutes unfettered autonomous human choice for human freedom in mutually responsible relationships."[39] The ELCA statement also specifically addresses disability as a social problem, arguing, "Society has a long history of mistreatment of people with disabilities, ranging from discriminatory to demeaning to even cruel. While there are exceptions, attitudes, laws, and practices in the United States have unnecessarily and unjustly restricted the opportunities of many people with disabilities to act on their own behalf and to contribute to society."[40] The statement connects this social and religious failure to concrete instances of discrimination, including in employment and education.

What is less clear in the ELCA and Catholic statements, and quite evident in the PC(USA) statement, is the extent to which the various denominations are successfully engaging people with disabilities in the formation of church policy, the creation of doctrine, and the provision of tools and resources to individual congregations. The PC(USA), both in its statement and in the materials provided for congregations, includes people with disabilities, scholars engaged in disability rights work, and people with training and experience in special education and other related fields as contributors to the content of the document. While the Roman Catholic and ELCA statements may follow this practice, if they do it is hard to see.

Church Participation by People with Disabilities

Although individual denominations do not appear to be tracking the participation of people living with disabilities in church communities, various other organizations interested in disability, and researchers of the quality of life for people with disabilities, are asking questions and gathering data about the degree to which people with disabilities are integrated into congregational life. Eiesland analyzes the statements of the early 1980s ALC, and argues that they were largely ineffective. Various denominations, as we have seen, have engaged in careful reflection on disability for many years. Have things changed since the 1970s and 1980s, or since the publication of *The Disabled God*, in terms of religious practice for people living with disabilities?

One important set of data on the lives of people living with disabilities is the ongoing study of Americans with disabilities created by the Kessler Foundation and the National Organization on Disability and conducted by Harris Interactive. The most recent Harris "Survey of Americans with Disabilities" was published in 2010, and reflected interview results with 1,001 adults with disabilities; the first was conducted in 1986. A total of six surveys have been completed. The content of the survey is wide ranging, and religious participation is studied and also indexed to other factors like income and access to transportation.

The Harris report data are not especially encouraging in terms of affirming the efficacy of denominational position statements to promote changes in congregational practice. Although the Harris study does not replace denominational self-study, it asks a set of questions about religious participation that help give a big-picture view of change since 1986. In short, although there has been significant movement on creating policy and theology to affirm people with disabilities, they are not coming to church in any greater numbers than in 1986. Although (as a recent Pew survey demonstrates) church attendance across the American population has declined modestly in recent years, this broad trend alone does not explain the relative lack of participation by people with disabilities.[41]

The most important piece of data in the Harris survey in terms of the issues posed in this chapter is the relationship between the rates of attendance at religious services for people with and without disabilities, what the Harris report calls the "gap." Significant gaps in the percentages of religious participation suggest that the disability itself is a factor preventing some people from religious participation who would otherwise be inclined (and this is contrary to what we might expect, if denominational outreach strategies and position statements were effective). The gaps between religious participation of people with and without disabilities are measurable and steady: over time, the average gap in the six survey years is 9.5 percent, with a low of 3 percent in 1998 and a high of 18 percent in 2000. So not only is religious service attendance declining slightly among people with disabilities, there is a measurable and steady difference between worship participation among people with disabilities and those without.

Framed partly in response to the Harris survey is the work of Melinda Jones Ault (whose research we began with), who along with Belva Collins and Erik Carter conducted a large-scale survey of parents of children with disabilities; she has published both qualitative and quantitative analyses, and a fuller picture emerges of the experiences of families of people with disabilities who are—or are not—participating in religious communities. Ault's study surveyed 416 parents with a child or children of any age with a disability who were or had previously participated in a faith community; she published the results in 2013.[42] Nearly 90 percent of the study's participants identified as Protestant or Catholic, so they correlate in a general sense with the denominations we have considered thus far.[43]

What was their experience at church? Ault writes,

> Parents did not perceive a high degree of supportiveness of including their
> sons or daughters within the places of worship they attended... . Almost
> one-third of parents reported having changed their place of worship because
> their child had not been included or welcomed; almost half had refrained
> from participating; more than half had kept their sons or daughters from par-
> ticipating in a religious activity because of a lack of support. ... Finally, more
> than half of parents reported that they had never been asked about the best
> way to include their sons or daughters in religious activities.[44]

This last data point is both remarkable and disheartening, and suggests a
significant failure to fulfill Eiesland's criteria of creating denominational
strategies on disability that have people with disabilities at the "speaking
center." This critique speaks to theological method as well as content. Even
if a denominational policy or statement on disability is theologically bril-
liant, if it is not created with the participation of people with disabilities
and effectively implemented to their benefit, it is performatively inadequate.

Conclusions

While, as we have seen in previous chapters, there is ample support in
the Christian tradition for recognizing the personhood and cultivating the
gifts of people with disabilities in congregations, and various denominations
are writing about disability, this has not translated to the presence of people
with disabilities in the pews. There is inequity in opportunity for participation and unease in some cases with the possibility of people with disabilities
taking on leadership positions or contributing to conversation, policy, and
strategy about their own presence in Christian churches.

Despite significant theological progress on the part of Roman Catholic
and mainline Protestant denominations, actual participation by people
living with disabilities in American churches is disproportionately low.
Individual churchgoers with children with disabilities report that they
are asked what they need from a congregation only about half the time.
The spirit of inclusion and transformation—at both the denominational
and the congregational level—may be willing, but the largely able-bodied
flesh remains weak. While church participation is not the only measure of
engagement with religious communities, it is an important indicator of the
success of efforts to reverse practices of exclusion of people with disabilities

from Christian life. As we saw in Chapter 5, seminary education that pre-
pares clergy for work with people with disabilities, and seminaries that are
accessible to people with disabilities, can help pave the way for more inclusive Christian congregations. In Chapter 7, we will turn to three examples
of Christian communities engaged in successful ministries to and for and
by people with disabilities.

CHAPTER SEVEN

Congregations and Ministry for People with Disabilities: Three Approaches

Introduction

Writer Reynolds Price, in his memoir *A Whole New Life*, describes the experience of being diagnosed with and treated for an aggressive spinal tumor that both endangered and eventually remade his life.[1] He does not sugarcoat or gloss over the details of the cancer's growth or his treatment, during which he suffered enormously; nor does he minimize the degree to which the experience of illness opened up for him new relationships and a different way of being himself. In his book, Price recounts in great and gracious detail the numerous friends, family members, and paid caregivers who helped him restructure his life during and after his treatment for his tumor. He tells of a vision he had of Jesus, "tall with dark hair, unblemished skin and a self-possession both natural and imposing,"[2] who gestures to Price in a dream, leading him into a lake. Echoing the biblical healing narratives, Price writes,

> Jesus silently took up handfuls of water and poured them over my head and back till water ran down my puckered scar. Then he spoke once—"Your sins are forgiven"—and turned to shore again, done with me. I came on behind him, thinking in standard greedy fashion, *It's not my sins I am worried about.* So to Jesus' receding back, I had the gall to say, "Am I also cured?" He turned to face me, no sign of a smile, and finally said two words—"That, too."[3]

What may be most striking about Price's memoir is his frank and unsentimental description of the challenges of his limited mobility and use of a wheelchair. He speaks to the isolation that many people with disabilities experience. Price writes,

> With all the fears of moving outside my own tight rooms, I also gave myself "practical" reasons for holding back from the outside world. My legs wouldn't get me out to the car, I still resisted the rented wheelchair, and I was months away from learning to deal with the potential daily bladder and bowel embarrassments to which the crippled are especially subject.... . And why force oneself on a world that's literally bent on repelling your presence and movement? As any cripple knows, the vast majority of American streets, houses, and commercial buildings still take the howlingly ludicrous view that no human being will ever live past the age of forty. In their architect's fantasy world, none of us will ever be slowed by age or illness, never be hobbled by arthritis or paralysis; and none of us, for whatever other thousand reasons, will someday be in serious need of the cooperation of bricks, concrete, and the watchful sympathy of able-bodied others.[4]

While Price does not specifically refer to churches as unwelcoming spaces, the clarity with which he describes the idealized able-bodied self and the overwhelming social expectations that most bodies will be that sort of body help illuminate the problem that many congregations find themselves having, and many people with disabilities find when engaging with typical congregations. Because ableism is so deeply ingrained a social norm, it is reflected in our architecture, our way of speaking to and about each other, our creation of our communities and schools and public spaces, our style of worship, our ways of imaging God, and our self-understanding as religious communities. His question is pointed and legitimate: why force yourself on a world, or congregation, that does not want you?

What responses can Christians give to this question? Moreover, what are Christians already doing in response to the reality Price describes? What are the characteristics of congregations that are engaged in successful, thriving ministries for, with, and by people with disabilities? When might a stand-alone congregation serve people's needs better than a ministry within an existing congregation? In this chapter we will examine the diverse approaches of three congregations from three different denominations, addressing three different types of disability.

As we consider how Christian congregations can effectively respond to the religious, social, and practical barriers that may prevent people with disabilities from participating in Christian communities, it is important to reflect on a few points. First, the concept of "inclusion," typically framed as a positive ideal for Christian churches, may be thornier than it first appears. Second, there are at least two approaches to creating accessibility within a congregation, and each has strengths and drawbacks; this chapter will summarize one and explore the other in depth. Finally, there is no one-size-fits-all strategy for effectively creating a disability-affirming community.

As we saw in Chapter 1, diversity is inherent in the concept of disability. Theologian Thomas Reynolds writes, "There is a kind of continuum on which all human abilities can be located, where shadings of grey eliminate dualistic distinctions between ability and disability. Human beings are limited and vulnerable, subject to the unpredictable contingencies of embodied existence, to become impaired, and ultimately to bodily deterioration and death."[5] In this array of embodied existence, people with a wide variety of impairments flourish, and the needs of these people vary as widely as their experiences of disability.

One strategy for insuring that people with disabilities can join, serve, and be served by Christian congregations is to focus on the congregation: on the accessibility of its building, the format, the schedule and pace of its worship and educational programs, the effectiveness of its commitment to identifying the needs and following the lead of individual members with disabilities, and so on. Another strategy, which may (as we will see below) emerge out of the first, is to create a ministry focused on a particular need. People with disabilities do not participate in Christian congregations at the rate that able-bodied people do. As we saw in Chapter 6, there are both practical and theological reasons for this pattern.

Inclusion and Deep Access

Reynolds argues for an approach he calls "deep access," rather than a standard model of inclusion, for Christian churches interested in becoming accessible to people with disabilities. He writes, "Put bluntly, efforts by non-disabled people to care for people with disabilities via welcoming and incorporating them in community life can—even with good intentions—be deceptively marginalizing, functioning implicitly as forms of exclusion."[6] He argues that the subjectivity and agency of people with disability can be compromised if the model for inclusion emphasizes care too strongly: if people with disabilities are regarded as passive recipients of care from able-bodied people, then a mutual and equitable community cannot form.

Instead of this model of "inclusion," Reynolds recommends what he calls *deep access*, which he says begins with "heeding provocation and imaginatively responding as if being called, invoked by the Spirit into a conversation that receives differences as a gift multiplying forms of bodily flourishing. Life in the shape of disability is a gift that can teach and empower faith communities."[7] Deep access, he says, involves a commitment both to the equality of all people and to the affirmation of real and meaningful differences between people and their experiences. This recognition of disability as an experience that *is* different from being able-bodied permits an honest approach to establishing social and religious access for all people. Thus, people with disabilities are not reduced to being static role models or objects of pity, but neither are the genuine needs for a reconfigured Christian community glossed over.

The Congregational Reform Model

How might congregations respond to the needs they see in their communities? One approach is to address the immediate context and practices of an individual congregation, and to ask: Can people with disabilities worship with this community? Is our building accessible? Do our music and our preaching reject the stigmas associating disability with sin? Do our programs offer flexibility for young people and adults with disabilities? Are we meeting the needs of the people in our congregation? How can we become not just open and inviting, but in practical and theological ways inclusive of people with disabilities who are not currently members of our church?

One excellent resource for individual congregations seeking to become more disability friendly is Erik Carter's book *Including People with Disabilities in Faith Communities: A Guide for Service Providers, Families, and Congregations*. He identifies many practical strategies for congregations to assess themselves and become, as he frames it, responsive to the needs of people with disabilities. Congregational leaders, parents, and anyone seeking a detailed guide to accommodation will be well served by his book.

Carter's book reflects many years of work in the field of special education; he earned his doctorate at Vanderbilt University and now teaches in the Department of Rehabilitation Psychology and Special Education at the University of Wisconsin-Madison.[8] His work reflects the best practices of special education programs and offers guidance for congregations interested in welcoming families living with disabilities. Particularly valuable are the checklists he offers for congregations to self-assess their level of current participation by people with developmental disabilities and the sample congregational outreach survey he provides for churches seeking to incorporate people with disabilities in the community into the life of their congregations. If a church community has identified a member whose needs are not being met, or has recognized that there is a gap between the experiences of disability among people in the community and the people in the pews, this book is an excellent resource for structuring congregational change.

The Focused Ministry Model

Once a congregation has begun to consider its response to people with disabilities, a larger, more organized and focused approach may emerge. In this chapter we will examine the diverse approaches of three congregations from three different denominations, addressing three different types of disability: one congregation has a mental health ministry, one congregation is a stand-alone Deaf church, and one congregation has a ministry for adults with intellectual disabilities. Some common threads will emerge, including the shared characteristic of distinction and specificity: each ministry developed organically within a community of Christians seeking to fill a gap in the local worship and fellowship experience, and seeking to affirm and support a particular group of people living with disabilities. Some central questions include the following: What was the impetus for each ministry? What resources did each congregation use in creating the ministry? In what sense is each congregation living out a Christian call? How does the ministry impact the members of the congregation and/or the participants? Each congregation has its own story of the origins of the ministry, its structure, and the underlying theological claims, and each provides a model for other Christian congregations interested in creating and sustaining similar ministries.

St. Joan of Arc's Mental Health Ministry

Origins

St. Joan's is a Catholic parish in Minneapolis, Minnesota, that has had a mental health ministry since 2006 and more recently has partnered with Bethlehem Lutheran Church, a nearby congregation, to provide a shared ministry to support mental health for members of the community.[9] The church's website describes the ministry: "St. Joan's Mental Health/ Mental Illness ministry provides a safe place of welcome for persons and families experiencing brain disorders. We work to educate, support and empower people with mental health challenges and to diminish the stigma surrounding mental illness. Because mental health issues are so critical to the broader community, our offerings are free and open to all."[10] The two congregations have been in collaboration for about four years.[11] The approach of this ministry is to network widely, drawing on the mental health support resources in the region and providing support and advocacy for ministry participants. For example, as part of the shared ministry, Bethlehem has begun a pilot program called Mental Health Connect, which includes a Mental Health Navigator, a trained professional who has an office at the church and offers support to people who need help accessing mental health care and to the families of people with mental illness. Bethlehem, St. Joan's, and other organizations and churches contribute to the funding of Bethlehem's Mental Health Connect ministry.[12] Both congregations emphasize that the mental health support services are not limited to Christians or to members of the two congregations, but are open to the community at large.

Structure and Theological Claims

As part of this collaboration, Bethlehem and St. Joan's take turns hosting a monthly social and educational ministry. On the second Monday of each month, the churches offer a program that begins with a light meal and a short inspirational reading or poem, followed by a range of speakers and events.[13] Thus, the gathering is not a Christian worship service, but it is structured like many Christian services are. This structure (rather than, for instance, a support group) helps the program emphasize mental health, rather than mental illness, and means that the ministry is open to anyone who wants to participate. The 2015 schedule, for example, includes sessions on nutrition and mental health, on parenting and on the needs of adolescents, on music, and two sessions geared specifically to be social events.[14] To keep the ministry balanced and welcoming, some sessions are focused on mental health specifically, and others are designed to be more social and to support the participants' overall wellness. Mary Ann Kelly-Wright, St. Joan's Pastoral Ministries director, says that between 20 and 50 people attend each monthly event. Some are members of Bethlehem or St. Joan's; some are people living with mental illness who are affiliated with neither congregation; some are families or friends of people with mental illness; others are healthcare professionals or pastors whose participation helps them provide support and care for the communities they work with.[15]

The networking emphasis of the shared ministry also benefits the congregations. This interaction between the congregations and the mental health ministry is key both for maintaining congregational support for the ministry and for establishing the mutuality of the relationship. For instance,

Sue Abderholden, the director of the Minnesota chapter of the National Alliance for Mental Illness (NAMI), was recently a pre-Mass speaker at St. Joan's, offering the congregation a chance to hear about mental health support systems in the state of Minnesota.[16] She spoke of mental health as a continuum, where people range from having "very good mental health to having a serious mental illness."[17] Abderholden emphasized the degree to which mental illness can disrupt a person's relationships, his or her ability to perform well at school or work, and his or her overall wellness. Like other disabilities, she argues, mental illness crosses gender lines and race and socioeconomic lines, and can affect people of any age. One barrier to getting support for maintaining mental health is the stigma associated with mental illness: Abderholden reminded her listeners that "even if intellectually we understand that it is an illness like any other, our actions don't reflect it."[18] She reviewed the history of responses to mental illness and educated the congregation about current approaches, thus providing information to the congregation and generating support for the monthly mental health ministry.

This mutuality illustrates one of the benefits that Reynolds identifies of recognizing the difference between disability and able-bodiedness. The participants in the mental health ministry are not the objects of charity for the congregation; instead, the ministry enhances the well-being of the congregation as well as those who attend the meetings. Reynolds writes that this is important "not only because such difference is often stigmatized and excluded, and not only because disability itself is diverse and not singular … but also because it is through such difference that relational interplay creatively negotiates communal life."[19] The varied experiences of the members of the congregations help shape and inform the mental health ministry, and focus on that ministry and its participants helps to build a thriving and healthy congregational life.

This sense of mutuality is also present in the ministry's relationships with the broader community. For example, one opportunity for Bethlehem and St. Joan's to partner with community efforts to increase mental health support in Minnesota came with the Twin Cities Public Television (TPT) campaign called "Make It OK," which focused on destigmatizing mental illness, making it easier for people to disclose their mental health needs. This served both to advertise the ministry to those outside the congregation who might benefit from it and to address the problem of religious teaching that harms people with mental illness. The congregation, and other Christians, benefit from this focus on how Christians can reframe their understanding of mental illness. Kelly-Wright and Daniel Abdul, a member of Bethlehem Lutheran, spoke on a television segment to publicize the ministry and to provide a voice for religious support of mental health care. Kelly-Wright said, "As people of faith ... we minister to people who have diabetes, who have heart disease, who may have a terminal illness; people with mental illness are another part of that, and need to be listened to and ministered to. We try to have resources for them, but basically to be present and to be a welcoming presence for them."[20] The host, half joking, replied that there is stigma within the church and that sometimes a religious response to a person with mental illness might be, "You just need a little more Jesus. That'll take care of your problem."[21] Kelly-Wright and Abdul laughed, and reiterated that their congregations provide a safe, welcoming space where, as Kelly-Wright put it, "the dignity of the human person is really recognized, no matter who you are or what you bring, and what struggles you have. It's also a social justice issue for most of us."[22] This social justice concern motivated the congregation to support the ministry, and there was no expectation that simply hearing the gospel would cure participants' mental health problems.

Successes and Challenges

Recognizing mental health stigma as a social justice issue is key. Kelly-Wright emphasizes that the issues facing people living with mental illness are not only about accessing health care. She describes problems for law enforcement in knowing how to constructively respond to mental health crises, problems of accessing insurance and paying for medication and heath care, job discrimination, poverty, and difficulty for people with mental illness in obtaining safe housing.[23] She points to Catholic social teaching as the underlying theological basis for St. Joan's interest in providing a mental health ministry. Kelly-Wright emphasizes especially the idea of the *Imago Dei* (here framed by the U.S. Conference of Catholic Bishops) as a social as well as a religious ideal: "Every human being is created in the image of God and redeemed by Jesus Christ, and therefore is invaluable and worthy of respect as a member of the human family. Every person, from the moment of conception to natural death, has inherent dignity and a right to life consistent with that dignity. Human dignity comes from God, not from any human quality or accomplishment."[24] Also central, she indicates, are the social teachings emphasized by the Catholic Charities of St. Paul and Minneapolis, including the doctrines of the dignity of the human person and the preferential option for the poor.[25]

One important theological issue for the mental health ministry is the clear distinction between illness and sin, particularly for people with mental illness who end their own lives. Kelly-Wright encourages the use of the term "completed" rather than "committed" suicide; the change in language helps to push back against the belief that mental illness is sinful. The congregation's position is that a person who completed suicide suffered from a disease, such as depression; he or she did not make a good decision. While in the past the Catholic Church had seen suicide as an offense, what is now appropriate is a compassionate response to the loved ones of someone who has completed suicide, or to the person himself or herself if the attempt is unsuccessful. People who have completed suicide, she says, can now typically be buried by the Catholic Church. While there are tensions and divisions around this issue, increasingly people who are suicidal are recognized as desperate, rather than lacking in moral fiber.[26]

Best Practices

The mental health ministry of St. Joan's and Bethlehem Lutheran has a number of strategic strengths that a congregation seeking to establish a similar ministry (for mental health or focused on another disability experience) could draw upon. First, the congregations have a well-established partnership, supported by each church and open to other congregations that want to participate. Some of the funding for the ministry is from external grants, and some is from ongoing support of the congregations. Second, the ministry is grounded in Christian theological claims and practices, but is explicitly and intentionally open to anyone. That "anyone" is further extended to mean not only "anyone with a mental illness" but "anyone seeking to support mental health." This double openness disentangles the practical support of the ministry from any particular affirmation of faith of participants, which might be a barrier for some people, and destigmatizes the participants by focusing on health, not illness. Finally, the ministry is grounded in the mental health support community of the region, and draws on resources and seeks partnerships with secular agencies and institutions. These relationships then flow back into congregational life and strengthen the congregation's bonds with the community. The primary goal is to support the mental health of the members of the broad community and to affirm their personhood and dignity, but an important secondary goal is to strengthen the Christian practice of the congregation, and to do so by engaging in partnership with the community, both ecclesial and secular. While this ministry is not focused on increasing the number of members of the participating congregations, it is an affirmation of belonging and an important support system for those who do worship at St. Joan's or Bethlehem.

Deaf International Community Church

There is an important disclaimer to be made with respect to the category of disability and the formation and identity of Deaf congregations. Many Deaf people do not identify as people with disabilities and instead recognize their language (American Sign Language in the United States) and culture, which flourishes in Deaf schools and churches, as a minority culture akin to the culture of a racial or ethnic minority group. This is in contrast to the way that Deaf people have regularly been classified and treated by hearing people in the United States. In including a Deaf congregation in this chapter, I am seeking not to undermine or set aside that important claim about Deaf identity but instead to explore the means by which Deaf people create and sustain their culture in a particular Christian religious setting. I am deeply appreciative of the hospitality shown to me by the Deaf church I visited during my research.

Origins

Deaf International Community Church (DICC) is a congregation located in Olathe, Kansas. Also in Olathe, located a few minutes outside of Kansas City, are the Kansas School for the Deaf[27] and the Deaf Cultural Center, whose mission is in part "to foster mutual understanding and cultural co-operation between deaf and hearing people. For our purposes, the word, deaf, includes people of all walks of life and all types of hearing loss."[28] This idea, that hearing people and Deaf people participate in different cultures, may be surprising to many hearing people. Marcel Broesterhuizen, a psychologist and theologian specializing in ministry with Deaf people, writes that for many Deaf people, being in community with other Deaf people is

> being with one's own people. With *this* people they share common experiences of communication problems and isolation (and with it a special sensitivity for the quality of relationships and contact), a common language (Sign Language), and their own way of life in a world filled with thinking in visual images. In this community with other Deaf people the concept of "disability" is far removed from their daily life experiences and is not a suitable description of their life.[29]

Unsurprisingly, this experience of being with one's own people is a rich and powerful cultural experience that is important in Deaf churches. Broesterhuizen relates the words of a member of one Deaf congregation: "Many Deaf Christians rejoice over their deafness in the knowledge that

God has singled them out for a special purpose. God has given them the ability to listen with their eyes and to perceive the beauty of His creation in a different light."[30] This is a rejection of the hearing understanding of deafness as a lack of capacity, and it is an embrace of the notion that God created some human beings Deaf, not as a punishment but as a gift.[31]

A Deaf church may or may not begin with the specific objective of affirming the culture and religion of Deaf Christians. In Kansas, DICC began as the ministry of a hearing church, and as the Deaf congregation grew, the members decided to establish themselves as a separate, independent congregation.[32] The pastor, Debbie Buchholz, describes some tension between the participants in the Deaf ministry and the hosting congregation: "The hearing church wanted them to remain a ministry and to remain 'under their care.' This meant that the deaf ministry was under the hearing deacon board and the hearing decided what to do with the tithe the deaf gave."[33] The Deaf congregation chafed at the experience of being supervised, but at that point were not yet financially independent of the hearing congregation.

This experience reveals a set of underlying historical issues for Deaf people. One of those issues is lack of access to highly paid professions. As Buchholz argues, the economic position the Deaf church found itself in is unsurprising since "many of the deaf earn minimum wages and cannot afford to 'tithe' each week and that meant they could not afford the pastor's salary or the bills that came with running a church. But … this became a sensitive topic for the [D]eaf [congregation]. We wanted autonomy. So we left and formed our own independent church."[34] The longstanding experience of marginalization of Deaf people in educational and professional settings has meant that the Deaf congregation had less economic power than congregations of hearing people typically do. According to data collected by the U.S. Census Bureau, income rates are lower and poverty rates are higher for people with disabilities, including people "experiencing deafness."[35]

Making a ministry/host church relationship more complicated, most Deaf people are born into hearing families, and thus many decisions about the education, socialization, language acquisition, medical interventions for, and religious upbringing of Deaf children are made by hearing parents rather than Deaf parents.[36] However, opportunities in the Deaf and hearing worlds for Deaf young people are increasingly prevalent; this includes opportunities within congregations. As Broesterhuizen argues, "Also in the life of the Church, Deaf people are ready to take their full place, not resigning themselves to the role of the disabled who are allowed to take silently their place at the banquet if they behave themselves properly.… . They also possess the same variety of priestly, prophetic, and kingly functions resulting from the priesthood of all baptized people."[37] The time of what he calls "spiritual colonialism ... during which dependence was supposed and fostered" is over.[38]

This approach, emphasizing the independence of the Deaf church, is evident at the DICC. Independent does not, however, mean separatist. The church's website reflects the diversity of upbringing and degree of deafness within the Deaf community; it describes the church's ministry as open to individuals who are Deaf or hearing: "Are you Deaf? ASL user? Oral user? Total communication user? Cued speech user? You've come to the right place. All of our worship services are in American Sign Language and professional voice interpreters are also available. We are very open to everyone and are more than willing to accommodate your needs."[39] This is reminiscent of Reynolds's description of deep access. He says that with deep access, "There is no inside-outside binary, but rather a roundtable gathering into which each guest is invited as host to one another, joined in relationships of mutual partnership and giving and receiving rather than dependency relationships of unilateral caregiving."[40] With this approach, the church has grown into a thriving community. Buchholz says, "The average size of a deaf church in the U.S. is 20–25 and we are currently serving about 275 people in our various ministries within our Deaf Church and Organization. We have been independent for five years."[41] The church provides a children's ministry and a youth ministry, and engages in local and global mission through its affiliation with Deaf International, a not-for-profit organization whose mission statement reads in part, "Deaf International is a community of Christians who desire to follow our Lord Jesus Christ in standing with the poor and oppressed by promoting human rights for Deaf people around the world and proclaiming the Good News of God's Kingdom in Deaf people's heart languages."[42] The focus of the mission work is thus for Deaf people to engage in religious and human rights work with other Deaf people.

Structure and Theological Claims

What is the worship service like at DICC? When I visited the congregation in August 2015, I was welcomed warmly. As a hearing person who does not speak ASL, I benefited from the ASL-to-English interpretation provided, and could see that a family comprised of Deaf and hearing people would all be able to worship at the church. Members of the congregation included Deaf people and hearing people. The service opened as many Christian services do, with contemporary Christian music playing over the speaker system while the lyrics to the songs were projected onto a screen at the front of the church. Volunteer leaders from the congregation signed the words in ASL along with the music at the front of the church. The service began with announcements, provided in ASL, in English interpretation, and projected onto the screen, and then moved to a testimony. The congregation sang two hymns, prayed, gathered an offering, and heard a children's sermon, a Gospel reading (also projected onto the screen), and a sermon, then Pastor Buchholz gave the benediction. Buchholz writes,

> The music is deaf friendly with visuals. Many [members] want only one song and some want three so we sing two. Music is an auditory pleasure and for those who cannot hear anything … it just isn't the same. So many do not like the music part but tolerate it because they feel that it is Biblical to sing praises to God on Sunday morning. We do have a big drum [and] we sing to the beat of the drum. That's more culturally fitting for the Deaf.[43]

This emphasis on cultural fit helps shape the sermon, as well. When she preaches, Buchholz keeps the Scripture text up on the screen so that the congregation can read along with her as she preaches on the text. She writes, "The sermons [I preach] are mostly expository so that they can see the verses being dissected and it gives [me an] opportunity to explain what the verses mean as we understand them."[44] This emphasis on the shared hermeneutic is important. As Kirk VanGilder's research indicates, Christian religious literacy among Deaf people is somewhat lower than among hearing peers.[45] Thus, the members of DICC may or may not be deeply familiar with the biblical texts; the expository preaching style is both preaching in the typical Christian sense and is also theological education, modeling for the congregation the practice of close reading and interpretation of the Bible.

This practice reflects a Deaf religious response to prevailing practices in hearing culture. Marcel Broesterhuizen argues that "From the first centuries of its existence the Church held that Deaf persons who were able to indicate by means of clear signs that they understood their meanings were admitted to the sacraments."[46] Despite this official policy, "practice was often different. In times when most Deaf children did not receive school education, Deaf people were often deprived of knowledge of the faith and they were not admitted to the sacraments…. Although school education has made faith more accessible for Deaf people, their participation in the faith community has remained far from easy."[47] Compounding the problem of access was the problem of interpretation; he argues that Christian biblical narratives typically reflect the point of view of able-bodied and hearing people, and (as we discussed in Chapter 2) thus reflect ableist biases. "No space is afforded for liberating the Bible stories from the perspective of the views on impairment and disability dominant in the cultural context when the Gospels were written."[48] Thus, the existence of Deaf churches provides Deaf people not only with a chance for accessible fellowship, and for culturally specific Christian practice, but also opportunities to engage in Deaf-specific interpretive practices.

Successes and Challenges

Buchholz is both pragmatic and hopeful about the situation of her congregation. On the one hand, the community is not yet financially robust, and Buchholz must be creative as she seeks resources to support the ministry. She relates,

> The church and all of the ministries are not able to support the finances that come with running a church. So the tithe monies [are] used to [pay] the bills and I have to raise my salary. It is very challenging, as I do not have insurance yet because I have to raise that too. Many times I have used my own money to pay for supplies.[49]

The choice between being an independent congregation and a sponsored ministry of another congregation, however, is clear. "If I take our church back to a hearing church, we lose our autonomy but I would receive full financial support. When you weigh the two, the autonomy wins... . I have had moments where I thought we couldn't remain an independent church but when I look at the benefits of providing the Deaf a Deaf church … I recover. It is good to be free!"[50] The cost of autonomy is financial security, but the price of security would be to lose some of the congregation's core practices.

The hope of the congregation, Buchholz says, is to have their own building some day. "Once a … group owns a building they have 'arrived' to the place of full autonomy. It is a time where we can announce to the world, 'we are here.' "[51] Their current situation, renting from a hearing congregation and accepting support from hearing congregations, is not perfect, but the Deaf congregation does have authority over its own financial decisions.

One other challenge for Deaf churches, Buchholz says, is something that Kirk VanGilder[52] emphasizes as well: a lack of trained Deaf religious leaders. Why is this the case? Buchholz says, "Maybe because the Deaf are still being denied equal access to education and maybe because there are not enough places for the Deaf to receive a Master's of Divinity. Education and money are probably two of the strongest reasons why we do not have enough Deaf pastors to do the work that needs to be done."[53] Broesterhui-zen describes this work in detail: in addition to leadership in congregational settings, there is a need for further translation of the Bible into ASL, devel-opment of Deaf liturgy for various denominations, and development of spe-cific religious signs to address gaps in ASL and other sign languages.[54]

Best Practices

Like St. Joan's, DICC is embedded in a larger community. The geo-graphical location of the church puts it in proximity to Deaf students and to people invested in the Deaf community. In addition, the congregation has ties to the larger Christian Deaf community; Debbie Buchholz's family includes Deaf members, including her son Noah, a pastor who is pursuing a Master of Divinity at Princeton and is currently planning a Deaf church in New Jersey; her son Jacob, who is hard of hearing, has finished his Master of Divinity at Princeton and is a pastor in Nebraska.[55] DICC's commitment to the broader community involves work with Deaf refugees, support of Deaf people in the region, and partnerships with other churches and organ-izations engaged in advocacy for Deaf people.

All of this work involves a culturally sensitive emphasis on autonomy rather than dependency, and explicit and intentional openness in response to broader cultural experiences of exclusion and segregation. Reynolds argues, "the community that we call church is a gift of the Spirit that traffics in differences, holding differences as gifts of grace."[56] Recognizing Deafness as a gift of grace, and responding to the need for Deaf-specific worship com-munities, DICC provides an invaluable church experience for Deaf people. Broesterhuizen points to a study that suggests that "the crucial factor in faith development is the degree to which Deaf people have access to faith knowl-edge."[57] This is the access that DICC provides.

Spirit Matters! at Rejoice! Lutheran Church

A third congregational ministry that offers a model for serving people with disabilities is called Spirit Matters!, hosted by Rejoice! Lutheran Church in Omaha, Nebraska. Spirit Matters! is a weekly gathering for adults with intellectual disabilities; participants gather for worship (including singing and prayer) in the church's sanctuary and then move to a large multipurpose area for organized activities, including crafts, games, karaoke, and dancing.[58] Volunteers of all ages are recruited from the congregation, and they receive training "to promote understanding of [the] participants and expectations."[59] The congregation has maintained accessible parking spaces, restrooms, and meeting space for the group, and other congregational ministries support Spirit Matters! by providing materials for crafts and musical performances.[60] Over the past several years, Rejoice! has welcomed me and many of my students; as part of our study of disability theology, we prepare for at least two volunteer sessions, come and participate in Spirit Matters!, and reflect on this experience. Many other volunteers participate in a similar capacity.

Origins

The ministry emerged from the needs of a member of the congregation. Cheryl Griess, who began the program, recalls that the son of a member had been in a car accident and experienced a brain injury. The father asked Griess, then the director of youth and family ministry at the congregation, what opportunities were available for his son. "I realized I didn't have anything to offer, so I met with our senior pastor and said, 'This is something we need to think about.' "[61] Griess worked to build the support of the congregation, and visited Bethel Lutheran Church in Middleburg Heights, Ohio, to learn about its similar program.[62]

Since its beginning 15 years ago, Spirit Matters! has expanded; the current coordinator, Carol Tillman, observed in 2013, "The program has grown enormously over the years. We started with twelve participants and [numbers have increased more than 10-fold]. These are participants as well as their caregivers. So if they live in a group home, a caregiver or two might bring four to six folks with them."[63] The program has become popular in the region and is a thriving ministry of the congregation.

Structure and Theological Claims

Spirit Matters! now serves upward of 150 adults with intellectual disabilities each week.[64] The music programming is particularly popular among participants, and is designed to offer multiple avenues for participation. The church's overview of Spirit Matters! explains:

> Christian music is presented by contemporary means with a leader who plays the guitar and sings using a sound system. Many of our participants join the leader in the front to sing and perform motions to the songs. We also supply the words to the music visually on a screen and encourage the use of simple shaker instruments to enhance each participant's experience. The importance of music to adults with [intellectual] disabilities cannot be underestimated.[65]

Key to the success of Spirit Matters! has been the ongoing participation of the congregation's youth and of other volunteers. As Tillman describes,

> [S]tudents going through our confirmation program can choose to partici-
> pate in this program once a month and serve in that way. That has led to
> some really neat things ... some of the kids, we've been doing this long
> enough now ... that we have kids that came through our program in middle
> school who are now seeking careers as advocates for people with special
> needs, because it made that much of a difference in their world.[66]

The church recognizes that this ministry is far from one-sided. This is an illustration of Reynolds's concept of deep access. He writes, "Deep love and fulfillment comes from being-with and witnessing each other's lives, learning from the gifts all bring to the table in different ways. This can build relationships of care and friendship, which means more than providing sim-ply the right to access."[67] Key to deep access is that the care and friendship are bidirectional: Spirit Matters! is not about people without disabilities serving people with disabilities but about shared fellowship.

This feature of the ministry was especially clear to me during a recent visit. I have taken classes to Spirit Matters! numerous times, including stu-dents enrolled in my recent Contemporary Christian Theology course. We came as volunteers, and brought several homemade carnival games with us. Two details of this particular visit stood out to me. First, a student from my class asked whether she could bring a friend who uses a wheel-chair; they knew each other from their days of military service. They arrived together, and as the students were setting up the activities that we had brought for the evening, a regular volunteer came to say hello to us. When he shook the hand of my student's friend, he welcomed him to the church. The young man responded warmly that he was very glad to be there *as a volunteer.* "Just like the rest of the kids, I'm here to help!" he said. He was not, as I could tell by watching him interact with the participants, distanc-ing himself from the people with intellectual disabilities who came regu-larly; he was instead emphasizing that he wanted to be recognized as capable of service.

The second moment that struck me that evening was when, after a lively worship service including songs and prayer concerns shared by partici-pants, organizer Carol Tillman announced that the student group was there for the evening. "Please make them feel welcome! Let them know we're glad to have them!" she enjoined. Numerous responses came from all over the sanctuary: "We will! We will!" And they did: the response to the students from the regular participants was enthusiastic and generous. Just like my student's friend, they wanted to be regarded as capable of hospitality. Each person in the room, whether a first-time visitor like my students, a regular participant, a volunteer from the church, or an invited guest, was called to the important work of engaging in ministry. In asking that we be welcomed, Tillman was emphasizing that the regular participants came not only to experience but also to extend to their friends and to new visitors the hospitality of the church community.

Successes and Challenges

One important aspect of training long-term volunteers at Spirit Matters! is describing and rejecting social stigma. The 2014–2015 Spirit Matters! training guide reminds volunteers, "Remember that these individuals have a long history of being stared at, ridiculed, and segregated from society. Treat adults as adults, regardless of the severity of their disabilities. Offer but don't force your assistance. Allow persons with disabilities to do things for themselves if they desire, even if it takes longer."[68] The training guide offers a brief summary of disability and disability-positive language, reminding volunteers, "people with disabilities are ordinary people with common goals for a home, job, and family.... Our participants love this program because they get to experience community with us and a large group of people just like them."[69] The training guide reminds the volunteers that because of the history of segregation of people with intellectual disabilities, participants may have "learned different rules by living in different environments."[70] Without reinforcing stereotypes, the training materials provide practical procedures for maintaining a comfortable setting for volunteers and participants alike: "Stay in main areas ... at all times; Pair up with ONE other confirmation student and work together; Dress casually and be well covered."[71] Everyone, visitor or participant or regular volunteer, wears a nametag to encourage good communication.

Like the mental health ministry at Saint Joan's, there is a positive and bidirectional relationship between Spirit Matters! and the congregation of Rejoice! Reflecting on this relationship, Tillman says,

> I want to tell you what a blessing the program has been to Rejoice!. Now I talked about the kids, and how important developing those things has been to them. But it has given Rejoice! a sense of mission in the community. I think we have seen how much and how gifted the people with special needs are. It's broadened our vision of how we can do ministry in the community, and we feel blessed to have the program here at Rejoice on a regular basis. I never, ever search for people [to volunteer at Spirit Matters!]. It just sort of

happens. We try not to advertise [for participants], because it's grown so much... . The support of our congregation, the community, and the people who volunteer in our program are so critical. It has been a really neat, neat program.[72]

The scale of the program is important. Tillman has restructured some aspects in response to the growing numbers. She says,

One of the challenges in our growth over the last few years is that the program has become less intimate, it's harder to get to know everybody, and feel like everybody is getting their needs met along the way. So we break down into small groups. They can choose from things like crafts or games, we might have speakers ... maybe making cupcakes or whatever it is we're doing for that evening... . And [the participants] really enjoy the small group activities.[73]

The mutuality and—as Tillman describes it—intimacy of the program, where each participant and each volunteer is known, is preserved by careful attention to the size of the program.

Best Practices

Like the mental health ministry of St. Joan's and Bethlehem, and DICC, Spirit Matters! stresses the well-being and agency of the participants in the ministry. Although some theologians of disability caution against emphasizing autonomy lest some people with disabilities be further marginalized, most human beings have and can express opinions about the choices that affect their well-being. Intellectual disability may leave some people particularly vulnerable to having their agency disregarded by others, and emphasizing the God-given dignity of each human being provides a religious and social model for supporting rather than supplanting each person's autonomy. The ministry of Spirit Matters! benefits the larger congregation by shaping behavior, modeling respect for all human beings, and offering an opportunity for fellowship between people with and without disability.

Also like St. Joan's and Bethlehem and DICC, Spirit Matters! is well networked in the larger community. Participants come from group homes and agencies in the region as well as private homes; the ministry has largely grown by word of mouth, and that informal network reinforces the well-being of many individuals who are not members of the congregation as well as many who are.

The ministry grew out of a need expressed by a member of the congregation, and the congregation took that challenge seriously. Financial support from the church is essential to Spirit Matters!, and strong emphasis on best practices for participants and volunteers alike have sustained the program. The emphasis on the benefit to the congregation as well as the participants reflects Reynolds's vision of deep access. He writes, "Vulnerability ... is an acknowledgement of the fact that human beings are exposed to and receive life from each other. It highlights the deep connecting points human bodies have with one another, points that indicate a basic web of mutual dependence.... . Vulnerability creatively holds together equality and difference, common sharing, and the gift of distinctiveness, and opens out into a relationship of interdependence."[74] Differences are not ignored or erased, but recede in significance, opening the way for fellowship.

Conclusions

The experience I had with my students visiting Rejoice! Lutheran is a small example of a significant phenomenon. One crucial aspect of congregational ministry to people with disabilities is to shift from the common goal of "including" people with disabilities in ministry to recognizing and cultivating the call to ministry of people with disabilities. As Reynolds argues, "If faith communities are about forming Christian care givers/ receivers who reflect God's compassionate attentiveness, there is a need for a radically different set of criteria to think about care than presently exists."[75] Such a spiritually healthy model of care is not yet universal.

Among the reasons that people with disabilities may struggle to find congregations that are accessible are the lack of training in disability for clergy and the lack of opportunity for people with disabilities to be trained in institutions of theological education. These are mutually reinforcing problems: if people with disabilities who are called to ministry do not have the support to discern and prepare for that call, and people with or without disability who are training for ministry also may not have the opportunity to learn the skills of creating a community that is open to people with disabilities, then individuals and families with disabilities will not find congregations able to serve them, and the potential for a person with a disability to have a supportive religious community as he or she responds to a call for ministry will be diminished.

The three communities that we have considered in this chapter offer distinctive and particular responses to Christian calls for fellowship. Each is different from the other in the set of people whose needs are being met by the community, in the structure and focus of the ministry, and in the impetus for the creation of the ministry. However, each has a set of shared characteristics that can serve as models for the deep access that Reynolds envisions: each community embraces the agency of those whom it serves, exists as a flourishing community where gifts are being recognized and cultivated and not a group of people who are the object of pity or one-sided care, is well integrated into a larger secular community, and provides a much-needed manifestation of Christian love and fellowship to all of those whom it serves.

CHAPTER EIGHT

Conclusions: What, Then, of God?

Conclusions

In Chapter 1, we examined the concept of disability and the task of disability theology. Throughout the book we have considered a variety of Christian theological responses to and constructs of disability: disability within the biblical tradition; the problem of construing Christian faith as primarily a cognitive experience, and possible responses to mental illness and suicide; the impact of historical discrimination against people with disabilities in the United States, and the possibility of constructive responses by faith communities; Christian leaders with disabilities; Christian theological accounts of disability and ecclesial responses; and finally, congregations engaged in ministries focused on people with disabilities.

A final important consideration remains: what can disability teach us about God? Theologian John Swinton evaluates the ways in which disability theology problematizes and destabilizes our understanding of human experience, and thus the established modes of using human experience to image God. He writes, "[M]ost influential theologians, historically and contemporarily have been able-bodied and have thus assumed an able-bodied hermeneutic as the norm for deciphering human experience and developing images of God."[1] Nonnormative bodily experiences have been "perceived as ... abnormality which, it is assumed, cannot reflect the true image of God."[2] This both reinforces the marginalization of people with disabilities and introduces a flawed and idolatrous tendency into Christian theology: the normate human body is wrongly reified.

Disability theology and ecclesiology provide a counterinterpretation of Christian practice and scripture; addressing problems with the normative view of disability opens up new ways to understand God. As Swinton writes, "[A] focus on disability challenges the church to see God for whom God is, return to its true character and engage in forms of life that are counter-cultural and faithful."[3] The work of the religious leaders profiled in Chapter 5 and the congregational ministries examined in Chapter 7 are examples of this phenomenon.

Swinton summarizes five images of God that have emerged in disability theology. One, developed by Nancy Eiesland, depicts God as disabled. Swinton sees Eiesland's model as overly dependent on sociological constructs and the language of disability rights and finds her emphasis on autonomy problematically exclusive. He writes, "People with advanced Alzheimer's disease, or those with profound intellectual disabilities i.e. people who are losing or do not have the very things that the disability studies approach seeks after, are necessarily excluded from the process."[4] Swinton has a fair critique of the set of assumptions Eiesland employs, but may in formulating it under-describe the importance of honoring the agency and cognitive capacity that any one human being does have. An intellectually disabled person, for instance, may not be capable of full comprehension of theological nuances, but if he or she has preferences about religious denomination, house of worship, mode of prayer, participation in religious sacraments, and so on, those preferences can and ought to be supported.

Swinton next describes the theological construct of God as accessible, described by Jennie Weiss Block. Of the inclusive model Weiss Block develops, Swinton observes, "Access and inclusion are important for faithful practice and it is the responsibility of religious communities to fulfill their calling in these areas."[5] Swinton argues that Weiss Block does not successfully engage with the disability rights perspective that undergirds Eiesland's work, revealing that the possibility of mutual conversation between disability rights and theology, where Christian theology not only is shaped by but also shapes secular discourse on disability, is limited. Thus, Weiss Block overestimates the value of mutual engagement between disciplines; as a result of this mistaken structural approach, Swinton argues, "Theology's public voice is invariably silenced if its dialogue partner is not participating in the conversation."[6]

Third, Swinton takes up Deborah Creamer's account of God as limited. Her argument extrapolates from human limits (part of every human being's experience, including people with disabilities) to a claim about divine limits. Swinton observes that this perspective is "in line with certain significant aspects of the Christian tradition,"[7] and he argues that Creamer does not mean for an account of God's limits to be exhaustively revelatory of all of God's nature.

The fourth, related theological claim about the nature of God that Swinton identifies is the description from Thomas Reynolds of God as vulnerable. Reynolds identifies interdependence and vulnerability as key features of human embodiment and of God incarnate. Swinton identifies Reynolds's theological method as similar to Weiss Block's and Creamer's in its critique of modernity and its emphasis on autonomy and capability. Reynolds, says Swinton, identifies the church as a locus of transformation where disability can be fully embraced.

Finally, Swinton takes up Stanley Hauerwas's description of God as a God who gives and receives. Hauerwas, Swinton argues, does not engage with a disability rights model at all, in contrast with many other theologians of disability. Like Swinton, who has written extensively on dementia, Hauerwas is interested in the experience of people whose capacities do not fit the model of modernity with its emphasis on cognition and capacity. "Hauerwas uses the experience of profound intellectual disability to draw our attention to a basic theological truth: we are *created* and as such, inherently *dependent*."[8] Swinton argues that this approach permits Hauerwas to reveal the illusions embedded in "the idea of independence and human autonomy."[9] Thus, Hauerwas can explore our created, vulnerable, dependent nature as human beings, and ask what this reveals about God.

Having engaged in this detailed analysis of prevailing theological positions on God and disability, Swinton offers his own constructive description. He observes that human beings are, in relation to God, neither disabled nor able-bodied, but "simply varied and loved."[10] He argues that disability in and of itself has no "specifically theological or moral significance.... As embodied beings *all people* are subject to the limits of biological existence, with its multiple variations and unpredictable outcomes."[11] Swinton sees the incarnation of God in Christ as the opportunity human beings have to get to know God, and argues that "Jesus' friendships were primarily with those who were rejected and marginalized."[12] Thus, he preserves the social justice emphasis of most strands of disability theology, while disavowing approaches like Eiesland's that argue for a God who is in some meaningful way participating in the experience of disability. Swinton responds to what he sees as the problematic modern emphasis on autonomy, capability, and cognition by arguing that "[t]o be loved by God and to receive that which the unknowable God chooses to offer is not an action dependent on capabilities; it is a gift given by God to human beings through the friendship of Jesus and mediated to all people through human friendship."[13] For Swinton, disability is not a feature of God, nor is it a barrier to religious participation for human beings.

Considering this thorough review of prevailing claims about God made by theologians of disability, we must ask: What does the research in this book suggest about the human experience of disability and the Christian understanding of God? How is God revealed in the various conversations and analyses of Scripture, politics, community life, and individual experiences of people with disabilities in the Christian community?

Chapter 1 provides an analysis of disability both as a widespread phenomenon and a marginalized experience, and—inasmuch as it is typically defined over and against able-bodiedness—as an unstable concept. The persistent and ongoing experience of disability among human beings, in its diverse manifestations, has by and large not been met by Christian communities with practices of welcome, of accommodation, of recognizing the value and gifts of people with disabilities. The critiques of scholars and theologians of disability illuminate the degree to which Christian churches have thus impoverished themselves and failed to live out God's call to form Christian community.

Chapter 2 takes up the problematic reality of the biblical texts that offer support for the personhood and agency of people with disabilities, but which also model their exclusion. Scripture both reinforces and undermines the association of disability with sin. If we are to read the Bible as a liberating text for people with disabilities, we must affirm God's goodness, God's creative power, and God's love for human beings. This entails developing a hermeneutic that critiques the claim that God rejects people with disabilities.

Just as the biblical texts tell us that humans are made in God's image, God also takes on human experience and from the recognition of Jesus as Christ Incarnate comes the revelation of God as present with human beings. In John 9, Jesus identifies the man born blind as a capable witness to Jesus's identity; he responds to the marginalization of the man by his social and religious community and identifies him as a locus of revelation of God's power and God's intention toward human beings. This modeling of communities of justice is also present in other biblical texts. Particularly in Paul's instructions to the church in Corinth, we see God as having created human beings as distinct individuals, each with the capacity to contribute to the life of the church.

In Chapter 3, we encounter a God who, as Luther argues, is able even after death to conquer evil and bring to peace and salvation a person who has completed suicide. When Luther writes to the Widow Margaret in the winter of 1528, he says, "Christ himself struggled like this in the Garden, yet he won the victory at last and was raised from the dead."[14] Luther emphasizes God's sovereignty over salvation, but also Christ's full, incarnate experience of despairing humanity. Swinton, in his discussion of dementia, provides a critique of the narrowness of the Christian theological tradition and offers instead a reminder that Jesus, on the cross, expressed his despair in the words of Psalm 22 and went on to provide a narrative of redemption.

Neither Luther nor Swinton describes a God whose power erases human fragility; both emphasize Jesus's full experience of human finitude.

Chapter 4, with its discussion of the difficult moral territory of eugenics, abortion, and the possibility of religious responses to families living with disability, suggests that God is the God who loves children born with disability and their families, affirms the capability of people with disabilities who are parents, and is present in sorrow with parents who choose to end a pregnancy because their unborn child's life will be painful, difficult, and short. Moreover, one clear role for church congregations emerges: they can support families, lift up the dignity of people with disabilities, and enrich their own communities by recognizing and responding to the opportunity to support people with disabilities. In other words, churches are called to model their responses to disability after God's own.

In Chapter 5, we see that God is a God who recognizes and calls God's people with disabilities to be leaders, from Moses to the present day, not in spite of who they are but because of who they are. Each of these narratives points us toward a more inclusive church and illuminates the possibility of fuller, richer religious life for Christians with and without disabilities. The church's growing capacity to nurture leadership among people with disabilities demonstrates the potential for fulfillment of the words of Jesus in John 9 and I Corinthians 12.

In Chapter 6, we explore the current theological work on disabilities offered by three denominations. This work is imperfect but it is ongoing and fruitful. God is the God who calls Christian churches to reflect on the human experience of disability and to continue to work to discover the Kingdom of God on earth. Churches increasingly have the tools to affirm the status of people with disabilities as beloved children of God and to create communities of justice, inside and outside the church.

In Chapter 7 we see that God is the God who is present in worship and fellowship with a range of communities serving a diverse set of needs. Reynolds offers the concept of deep access, and each profiled congregation embodied one community responding to a specific set of needs. St. Joan of Arc's mental health ministry partnership not only provides support for individuals with mental illness, their families, and their care providers, but also gives out a call to publicly reject the stigmas associated with mental illness. The Deaf International Community Church recognizes the importance of a worship community fluent in American Sign Language and attuned to the cultural and theological practices of Deaf people. Spirit Matters! at Rejoice! Lutheran Church provides an opportunity for worship, fellowship, and friendship among people with and without disabilities, and continues to shape the life of the congregation. In each of these contexts, the divine call to open, affirming, justice-seeking community is embodied.

What does this set of observations, testimonies, and analyses suggest about the nature of God? Swinton argues that "[t]he incarnation, cross, and resurrection of Jesus indicate strongly that God is deeply implicated in both the suffering and the joy of human existence and the world. As Dietrich Bonhoeffer put it, 'Only the suffering God can help.' "[15] While disability may or may not involve suffering at any given moment, just like other experiences of human embodiment, Swinton's point about God's presence in both suffering and joy is key. Disability as an umbrella term for a rich diversity of bodily experience is an unstable concept, but it is an experience for which God is present in every single instance. The miracle of Jesus Christ is not in his healing of individual people, but in his presence with us, both divine and human. Jesus's particular experience of crucifixion and resurrection, his despair, his loneliness facing death, and his examples during his ministry of restoring marginalized people to dignity and religious and social standing offers Christian churches what we need to respond to the phenomenon of disability: evidence that God is with us and calls us to rearrange and restructure our communities into richer and fuller embodiments of the Kingdom of God. God is the God of omnipresence, who is with us and is calling us into community with each other.

Notes

Chapter One: Introduction to Disability Theology

1. Thomas Reynolds, *Vulnerable Communion*. Nashville: Brazos Press, 2008, p. 38.

2. Lennard Davis, *Bending Over Backwards: Disability, Dismodernism & Other Difficult Positions*. New York: NYU Press, 2002, p. 50.

3. Ibid., p. 41.

4. Ibid., p. 87.

5. Ibid., p. 37.

6. As an aside, in this book I attempt to honor and explore the claim of Deaf people to a cultural identity by including a Deaf scholar of religion and a Deaf congregation in my discussion of religious leaders and communities. Thus, I must acknowledge that discussing Deafness in a book with "disability" in the title also implicitly affirms the classification of Deaf people as people with disabilities. On balance, it seemed a better choice to risk offense by reiterating the classification mistake than to exclude discussion of Deafness from the book entirely.

7. "Introduction to the ADA." http://www.ada.gov/ada_intro.htm

8. http://www.justice.gov/sites/default/files/crt/legacy/2010/12/15/tal057.txt

9. John Swinton, "Theologies of Disability: Challenges and New Possibilities," *International Journal of Practical Theology*, 14:2, January 2001, p. 280.

10. Deborah Creamer, "Made in the Image of God: Rethinking Accessible to All," Lecture delivered at Lancaster Theological Seminary, April 16, 2015. https://lancasterseminary.edu/multimedia

11. John Lee Clark, *Where I Stand: On the Signing Community and My DeafBlind Experience* (Kindle Location 1516–1519). Minneapolis: Handtype Press, 2014.

12. Craig Satterlee, "Learning to Picture God from Those Who Cannot See," *Homiletic*, 36:1, 2011, p. 54.

13. Reynolds, *Vulnerable Communion,* p. 40.

14. Davis, *Bending Over Backwards,* p. 23.

15. Ibid.

16. Gustavo Gutiérrez, *A Theology of Liberation.* Maryknoll, NY: Orbis Books, 1988, p. 24.

17. William M. Ramsey, *Four Modern Prophets.* Louisville: Westminster John Knox, 1986, p. 53.

18. "Remembering the Poor: An Interview with Gustavo Gutiérrez," *America: The National Catholic Review,* February 3, 2003. http://americamagazine.org/issue/420/article/remembering-poor-interview-gustavo-gutirrez

19. Clark, *Where I Stand* (Kindle Location 860).

20. Swinton, "Theologies of Disability," pp. 274–275.

21. Paul Tillich, "On Healing," *The New Being,* Lincoln, NE: Bison Books, 2005, p. 37.

22. Paul Tillich, *Systematic Theology III.* Chicago: The University of Chicago Press, 1976, p. 280.

23. As I learned, this included unloading the dishwasher, doing laundry, gardening and cutting the grass, feeding the cats, and many other household tasks. I needed a great deal of help to care for my household and my children. Many people in my congregation, Augustana Lutheran Church in Omaha, Nebraska, offered us support and help, which was instrumental in my recovery.

Chapter Two: Fruitful Reading of Scripture

1. Rebecca Raphael, *Biblical Corpora: Representations of Disability in Hebrew Bible Literature.* London: Bloomsbury, 2008, p. 139.

2. Ibid., p. 15.

3. The book does not take up issues of disability, but it includes liberation theologies from many other social and cultural contexts.

4. Anthony Pinn, ed., *Liberation Theologies in the United States.* New York: New York University Press, 2010, p. 1.

5. This issue is an ongoing interpretive problem for many Christians: consider, for instance, biblical texts that support slavery, or the exclusion of women from religious leadership, or support capital punishment for adultery, or texts that affirm a divinely established monarchy, or polygamous marriage; for the most part, modern mainline Christians do not hold those texts as normative for the social or political or family structures of their world.

6. Kathy Black, *A Healing Homiletic: Preaching and Disability.* Nashville: Abingdon Press, 1996, p. 20.

7. Thomas Reynolds, *Vulnerable Communion.* Grand Rapids: Brazos Press, 2008, p. 35.

8. Raphael, *Biblical Corpora,* p. 138.

9. Ibid.

10. Nancy Eiesland, *The Disabled God: Toward a Liberatory Theology of Disability.* Nashville: Abingdon Press, 1994, p. 72.

11. Ibid., p. 70.

12. See John 5:15, for example: "Later Jesus found him in the temple and said to him, 'See, you have been made well! Do not sin any more, so that nothing worse happens to you,'" and Exodus 4:11, "Then the Lord said to him, 'Who gives speech to mortals? Who makes them mute or deaf, seeing or blind? Is it not I, the Lord?" See also Leviticus 21, discussed later in the chapter.

13. Amos Yong, *The Bible, Disability, and the Church*. Grand Rapids: Eerdmans, 2011, p. 26.

14. Black, *A Healing Homiletic*, p. 12.

15. Ibid.

16. Ibid., pp. 12–13.

17. Ibid., p. 51.

18. Ibid., p. 119.

19. Yong, *The Bible, Disability, and the Church*, p. 7.

20. Ibid., p. 23.

21. Rebecca Raphael notes that the punishments God imposes on Adam and Eve and the serpent, after the Fall, are "disabling," at least to Eve and the serpent, whose ability to walk is removed. Raphael writes of Eve, "Increased birth-pangs hamper the body in its former ability, and are thus disabling—as much as one would dare with a character who is the first mother" (Raphael, *Biblical Corpora*, p. 56).

22. Reynolds, *Vulnerable Communion*, p. 186.

23. Ibid., p. 60.

24. Colleen Grant, "Reinterpreting the Healing Narratives," Nancy L. Eiesland and Don E. Saliers, eds. *Human Disability and the Service of God*. Nashville: Abingdon, 1998, p. 79.

25. Ibid., p. 80.

26. Ibid.

27. Ibid., p. 81.

28. Ibid., p. 83.

29. Jennie Weiss Block, *Copious Hosting*. New York: Continuum, 2002, p. 153.

30. Black, *A Healing Homiletic*, p. 48.

31. Raphael, *Biblical Corpora*, p. 38.

32. Yong, *The Bible, Disability, and the Church*, p. 20.

33. Sarah Melcher, "Visualizing the Perfect Cult," Nancy L. Eiesland and Don E. Saliers, eds. *Human Disability and the Service of God*. Nashville: Abingdon, 1998, p. 57.

34. Ibid., p. 61.

35. Ibid., pp. 65–66.

36. Ibid., p. 69.

37. Ibid.

38. Although in II Corinthians 12:5–10, Paul writes about his own experience of a "thorn in the flesh," sometimes taken to be a description of bodily disability, a full discussion of Paul's possible identity as an apostle with a disability is outside the scope of this chapter.

39. Brian Brock, "Theologizing Inclusion: 1 Corinthians 12 and the Politics of the Body of Christ," *Journal of Religion, Disability & Health*, 15:4, 2011, p. 352.

40. Ibid., p. 368.
41. Ibid., p. 361.
42. Ibid., p. 372, n5.
43. Yong, *The Bible, Disability, and the Church*, p. 93.
44. Ibid., p. 95.

Chapter Three: Self, Faith, and Christ: Questions of Suicide and Dementia

1. *Luther,* directed by Eric Till. Beverly Hills, CA: Metro-Goldwyn-Mayer Studios, 2003. DVD.
2. Ibid.
3. Ibid.
4. I am presuming in this chapter that mental illness and dementia are disabilities. See Chapter 1 for a discussion of the complex problem of defining disability.
5. An important caveat is that not all people who commit suicide have a mental illness, and certainly not every person with a mental illness experiences suicidal ideation.
6. John Swinton, *Dementia: Living in the Memories of God.* Grand Rapids: Eerdmans, 2012, p. 197.
7. Jeffrey Watt, *Choosing Death, Suicide and Calvinism in Early Modern Geneva.* Kirksville, MO: Truman State University Press, 2001, p. 53.
8. Swinton, *Dementia,* p. 112.
9. Ibid., p. 205.
10. Ibid., p. 161.
11. Ibid., p. 201.
12. Theodore Tappert, ed. and trans., *Luther: Letters of Spiritual Counsel.* Louisville, KY: Westminster John Knox, 1955, p. 59.
13. Ibid.
14. Ibid.
15. Watt, *Choosing Death,* p. 255, n10.
16. H. C. Erik Midelfort, "Religious Melancholy and Suicide," *Madness, Melancholy, and the Limits of the Self.* Graven Images, Madison: University of Wisconsin Law School, 1996, p. 45.
17. Tappert, *Luther.* p. 59.
18. Ibid.
19. This language from the psalm is evocative of his suggestion in the Table Talk, discussed below, that human beings are actually "dispatched" by God. (Martin Luther, *Luther's Works: Table Talk*, Volume 54. Philadelphia: Fortress Press, 1967, p. 29.)
20. Luther, *Luther's Works.*
21. Ibid., p. 29.
22. Watt, *Choosing Death,* p. 78.
23. Midelfort, "Religious Melancholy and Suicide," p. 42.
24. Ibid., p. 43.

25. Luther, *Luther's Works,* p. 29.

26. Midelfort, "Religious Melancholy and Suicide," p. 45.

27. Tappert, *Luther,* p. 89.

28. Ibid.

29. Ibid.

30. Ibid., p. 90.

31. Ibid.

32. Ibid., p. 91.

33. Ibid.

34. Ibid., p. 84.

35. Ibid., p. 85.

36. Ibid.

37. Ibid.

38. Ibid., p. 86.

39. Ibid.

40. Ibid., p. 87.

41. My thanks to Vitor Westhelle for the excellent suggestion to reframe the idea of the demonic in Luther's argument about suicide as the mistaken belief that standard cognition is necessary for salvation.

42. Kerry Weber, "Religion Update Fall 2012: In Profile," *Publishers Weekly,* August 2012, p. 12.

43. Swinton, *Dementia,* p. 281.

44. Ibid., p. 10.

45. Ibid., p. 24.

46. Ibid., p. 281.

47. Ibid.

48. Ibid., p. 267.

49. Ibid.

50. Similarly, infants are baptized prior to gaining the capacity to understand who God is, read the Gospels, or participate in Christian community, but their undeveloped faith does not strike us as endangering their salvation. My thanks to Vitor Westhelle for that insight.

Chapter Four: Feminism, Reproductive Rights, and Disability: Conflicting Accounts of Autonomy

1. Emily Rapp, "Rick Santorum, Meet My Son," *Slate,* February 27, 2012. http://www.slate.com/articles/double_x/doublex/2012/02/rick_santorum_and_prenatal_testing_i_would_have_saved_my_son_from_his_suffering_.html

2. Emily Rapp, *Poster Child.* New York: Bloomsbury, 2007, p. 10.

3. Ibid.

4. Ibid., p. 11.

5. Ibid.

6. http://palmdesertmfa.ucr.edu/faculty/

7. Emily Rapp, "A New Baby Doesn't, and Shouldn't, Replace What's Lost," *The New York Times,* March 13, 2014. http://parenting.blogs.nytimes.com/2014/03/13/dragon-mother-emily-rapp-a-new-baby-doesnt-and-shouldnt-replace-whats-lost/?_r=0

8. Rapp, "Rick Santorum, Meet My Son."

9. Brian Montopoli, "UN Treaty on Disabilities Falls Short in Senate," CBS News, December 4, 2012. http://www.cbsnews.com/news/un-treaty-on-disabilities-falls-short-in-senate/

10. In this section of the chapter I have revised and updated "Valuing All Human Beings: Disability and Reproductive Rights Meet Congress," originally published on January 24, 2013, in *Sightings,* the online journal of the Martin Marty Center at the University of Chicago Divinity School.

11. "Convention on the Rights of Persons with Disabilities," Article 1. http://www.un.org/disabilities/convention/conventionfull.shtml

12. http://www.un.org/disabilities/

13. http://www.un.org/disabilities/convention/conventionfull.shtml

14. Nancy L. Cohen, "Christian Right Enforces GOP Senators' Vote against UN Disabilities Treaty," *The Guardian*, December 6, 2012. http://www.theguardian.com/commentisfree/2012/dec/06/christian-right-republican-senators-disabled-rights-treaty

15. http://www.aapd.com/what-we-do/interfaith/is%20http:/www.aapd.com/what-we-do/interfaith/faith-community-support-for.pdf

16. "NCD Statement on the Convention on the Rights of Persons with Disabilities (CRPD)," July 4, 2014. http://www.ncd.gov/publications/2014/07142014/

17. Cohen, "Christian Right Enforces GOP Senators' Vote."

18. "Santorum: U.N. Disabilities Treaty Would've Had Bureaucrats Unseat Parents," The Daily Beast, December 5, 2012. http://www.thedailybeast.com/articles/2012/12/05/santorum-un-disabilities-treaty-would-ve-had-bureaucrats-unseat-parents.html

19. Rich Santorum, "Problematic Disabilities Treaty up for Consideration Again," *Roll Call*, August 4, 2014. http://www.rollcall.com/news/Rick-Santorum-CRPD-and-his-daughter-Bella-235504-1.html

20. http://www.lifenews.com/2012/12/04/u-s-senate-defeats-crpd-treaty-that-would-promote-abortion/

21. Paul A. Lombardo, *Three Generations, No Imbeciles* (Kindle Location 5110). Baltimore, Maryland: Johns Hopkins University Press, 2010.

22. Ibid., Chapter 8.

23. Ibid. (Kindle Location 2522).

24. Ibid. (Kindle Location 2545).

25. Ibid. (Kindle Location 192).

26. Ibid. (Kindle Location 1197).

27. Ibid. (Kindle Location 4433).

28. Ibid.

29. Rosalind Hursthouse, "Virtue Theory and Abortion," Perry, Bratman, and Fischer, eds. *Introduction to Philosophy: Classical and Contemporary Readings.* Oxford: Oxford University Press, 2007, pp. 592–606.

30. Erik Parens and Adrienne Asch, "Disability Rights Critique of Prenatal Genetic Testing: Reflections and Recommendations," *Mental Retardation and Developmental Disabilities Research Reviews*, 9, 2003, p. 41.

31. Ibid., p. 42.

32. Nancy Eiesland, *The Disabled God.* Nashville, Tennessee: Abingdon Press, 1994, p. 23.

33. Adrienne Asch, "Prenatal Diagnosis and Selective Abortion: A Challenge to Practice and Policy," *American Journal of Public Health*, (89)11, 1999, p. 1650.

34. Ibid., p. 1651.

35. National Council on Disability, "The Impact of Disability on Parenting," *Rocking the Cradle: Ensuring the Rights of Parents with Disabilities and Their Children,* 2012. https://www.ncd.gov/publications/2012/Sep272012/Ch12

36. Ibid.

37. Suzanne Smeltzer, "Pregnancy in Women with Physical Disabilities," *Journal of Obstetric, Gynecologic, and Neonatal Nursing*, 36(1), January/February 2007, p. 88.

38. Ibid.

39. Ibid., p. 90.

40. Robyn Powell, "Can Parents Lose Custody Simply Because They Are Disabled?" *GPSolo*, 31(2), March/April 2014, p. 15.

41. Ibid.

42. U.S. Court of Appeals for the Eighth Circuit, "MKB Management Corp., Doing Business as Red River Women's Clinic; Kathryn L. Eggleston, M.D." http://sblog.s3.amazonaws.com/wp-content/uploads/2015/07/ndopinion.pdf

43. John Swinton, *Dementia.* Grand Rapids, Michigan: Eerdmans, 2013. p. 131.

44. Harriet McBryde Johnson, "Unspeakable Conversations," *The New York Times,* February 16, 2003.

45. Ibid.

46. This position is more fully developed in Singer's own writing, including his 2009 *New York Times* essay "Why We Must Ration Health Care."

47. Johnson, "Unspeakable Conversations."

48. Ibid.

49. Eiesland, *The Disabled God,* p. 77.

50. Tamar Lewin, "Ohio Bill Would Ban Abortion If Down Syndrome Is Reason," *The New York Times*, August 22, 2015. http://www.nytimes.com/2015/08/23/us/ohio-bill-would-ban-abortion-if-down-syndrome-is-reason.html?_r=0

51. Amy Julia Becker, "North Dakota's Abortion Ban Is a Bad Way to Stop Selective Abortion," *The Atlantic*, April 2013.

52. Ibid.

53. Piepmeier is quoting State Representative Bette Grande, who in turn is quoted by the *New York Times* on March 26, 2013, in a story entitled "New Laws

Ban Most Abortions in North Dakota," and in a March 26, 2013, article in LifeNews.com entitled "North Dakota Now First State to Ban Abortions Based on Down Syndrome." http://www.nytimes.com/2013/03/27/us/north-dakota-governor -signs-strict-abortion-limits.html.

54. Becker, "North Dakota's Abortion Ban."

55. Ibid.

56. Johnson, "Unspeakable Conversations."

57. Parens and Asch, "Disability Rights Critique of Prenatal Genetic Testing."

58. Ibid.

59. Caeton, D. A., "Choice of a Lifetime: Disability, Feminism, and Reproductive Rights." *Disability Studies Quarterly,* 1(11), 2001, p. 8.

60. We will revisit this process in Chapter 7.

61. Dov Fox et al., "Disability-Selective Abortion and the Americans with Disabilities Act," 2009, Faculty Publications, Paper 1240. http://scholarship .law.wm.edu/facpubs/1240, p. 865.

62. Asch, "Prenatal Diagnosis and Selective Abortion," p. 1655.

63. Eiesland, *The Disabled God,* p. 93.

Chapter Five: Recognizing Voices, Honoring Testimony

1. Deborah Creamer, "Theological Accessibility: The Contribution of Disability," *Disability Studies Quarterly,* 26:4, Fall 2006. http://dsq-sds.org/article/view/812/987

2. Creamer, "Made in the Image of God: Rethinking Accessible to All," Lecture delivered at Lancaster Theological Seminary, April 16, 2015. https://lancaster seminary.edu/multimedia

3. Creamer, "Theological Accessibility."

4. Albert Herzog, "We Have This Ministry: Ordained Ministers Who Are Physically Disabled," Nancy L. Eiesland and Don E. Saliers, eds., *Human Disability and the Service of God.* Nashville: Abingdon, 1998, p. 187.

5. Creamer, "Made in the Image of God."

6. https://www.gallaudet.edu/hprs/faculty_-_staff/history_philosophy_religion _and_sociology/religion/vangilder_kirk.html

7. See Chapter 7 for additional discussion of this position.

8. Robert L. Walker, *Speaking Out: Gifts of Ministering Undeterred by Disabilities.* CreateSpace Independent Publishing Platform, 2012, p. 34.

9. In 1988, the Deaf President Now movement began at Gallaudet University when a hearing president was chosen for the school. According to the summary on Gallaudet's website, "Deaf President Now (DPN) has become synonymous with self-determination and empowerment for deaf and hard of hearing people everywhere." http://www.gallaudet.edu/dpn-home.html

10. Walker, *Speaking Out,* pp. 34–35.

11. Interview, February 13, 2015.

12. Ibid.

13. Ibid.

14. Ibid.

15. VanGilder notes, "The Student Forum was another program of the General Board of Higher Education and Ministry, and became the forerunner to the rebirth of the United Methodist Student Movement a few years later, in part due to the energy of my cohort of college aged United Methodists" (Walker, *Speaking Out*, p. 36).

16. Ibid., p. 37.

17. Ibid.

18. Ibid., p. 30.

19. Interview, February 13, 2015.

20. Ibid.

21. Ibid.

22. Author of *A Healing Homiletic: Preaching and Disability*, discussed in Chapter 2.

23. Walker, *Speaking Out*, p. 38.

24. Ibid., p. 39.

25. Ibid.

26. VanGilder, email, March 10, 2015.

27. Erin M. Diericx, "The Calling," God the Healer. http://god-the-healer.com/the-calling/calling-ediericx/

28. Interview, April 24, 2015, and October 16, 2015.

29. Diericx, "The Calling."

30. Interview, February 26, 2015.

31. Diericx, "The Calling."

32. Ibid.

33. Interview, April 24, 2015.

34. Ibid.

35. Diericx, "Bringing People of All Abilities Together," God the Healer. http://god-the-healer.com/2015/05/24/bringing-people-of-all-abilities-together/

36. Ibid.

37. Ibid.

38. Ibid.

39. Diericx, "Breaking Down Boundaries," God the Healer. http://god-the-healer.com/2015/05/10/breaking-down-boundaries-physcial-psychosocial-and-spiritual/

40. Ibid., quoting Nancy Eiesland, *The Disabled God*, p. 109.

41. Ibid.

42. Diericx, "Cerebral Palsy Is a Blessing," God the Healer. http://god-the-healer.com/2015/03/25/cerebral-palsy-is-a-blessing/

43. Ibid.

44. Ibid.

45. Ibid.

46. "About Craig." http://craigasatterlee.com/about-craig.html

47. Interview, February 20, 2015.

48. Ibid.

49. Ibid.
50. Ibid.
51. Ibid.
52. Ibid.
53. Ibid.
54. Craig Satterlee, "Indeed, Bishop Satterlee Is Legally Blind," p. 1. http:// craigasatterlee.com/yes-craig-is-blind.pdf
55. Ibid.
56. Satterlee, " 'The Eye Made Blind': The Language of Disability in Worship," *Liturgy*, 25:2, 2009, p. 38.
57. Ibid., p. 34.
58. Ibid., p. 33.
59. Ibid., p. 36.
60. Satterlee, "Indeed, Bishop Satterlee Is Legally Blind," p. 2.
61. Satterlee, "Learning to Picture God from Those Who Cannot See," *Homiletic*, 36:1, 2011, p. 51.
62. Ibid.
63. Ibid.
64. Ibid, p. 49.
65. "Biographical Sketch," *UBE: Purple Yam*. http://ube-purpleyam .blogspot.com/p/biographical-sketch.html
66. Ibid.
67. Fry Brown, *Weary Thrones and New Songs*. Nashville: Abingdon, 2002, p. 43.
68. Email interview, April 13, 2015.
69. Ibid.
70. Ibid.
71. Raedorah Stewart, "Made by God, Broken by Life: Developing an African American Hermeneutic for Disability," *Tikkun*, November 7, 2014. http:// www.tikkun.org/nextgen/made-by-god-broken-by-life-developing-an-african -american-hermeneutic-for-disability
72. Ibid.
73. Ibid.
74. Email interview, April 13, 2015.
75. Stewart, "What Is 'the Egypt United Methodist Church?' " Sermon delivered January 16, 2011. http://www.bloominthedesert.org/voiceswritings.html
76. Ibid.
77. Stewart, "Made by God."
78. Ibid.
79. Ibid.
80. Ibid.
81. Ibid.
82. Ibid.
83. Creamer, "Theological Accessibility."

Chapter Six: Disability in the Contemporary Church: Social Statements and Denominational Practice

1. Melinda Jones Ault, Belva C. Collins, and Erik W. Carter, "Factors Associated with Participation in Faith Communities for Individuals with Developmental Disabilities and Their Families," *Journal of Religion, Disability, and Health,* 17:2, 2013, p. 203.

2. Nancy Eiesland, *The Disabled God: Toward a Liberatory Theology of Disability.* Nashville: Abingdon Press, 1994, p. 69.

3. Ibid., p. 75.

4. Ibid., p. 76.

5. *1980 Reports and Actions of the Tenth General Convention of the American Lutheran Church,* p. 710.

6. Ibid.

7. Eiesland, *The Disabled God,* p. 76.

8. "Lutherans Drop Plan to Bar Disabled Clergy," *The New York Times,* September 12, 1985. http://www.nytimes.com/1985/09/12/us/lutherans-drop-plan-to-bar-disabled-clergy.html?.html

9. "Seminary Admission and Certification Criteria in Relation to the Work ALC Pastors Are Expected to Do." Agenda Exhibit T-1, American Lutheran Church, Church Council Minutes, June 3–7, 1985.

10. Ibid., p. 2.

11. Email, Ronald Duty, April 23, 2015.

12. Eiesland, *The Disabled God,* p. 76.

13. Ibid., p. 77.

14. Duty, p. 3.

15. Eiesland, *The Disabled God,* p. 77.

16. Ibid.

17. Email, Ronald Duty, April 23, 2015.

18. Naomi Annandale and Erik Carter, "Disability and Theological Education: A North American Study," *Theological Education,* 8:2, 2014, p. 86.

19. ATS policy guideline, p. 14.

20. Annandale and Carter, "Disability and Theological Education," p. 92.

21. Ibid.

22. Ibid.

23. Ibid., p. 83.

24. Ibid., p. 91.

25. Ibid., p. 83.

26. "Disability and Theological Education," *Association of Theological Schools Policy Guidelines,* p. 13. http://www.ats.edu/uploads/about-ats/documents/policy-guideline-disability-and-theological-education.pdf

27. Many other denominations also have explicit theological positions on disability and resources for congregations; considering them all is outside the scope of the current conversation.

28. *Pastoral Statement of U.S. Catholic Bishops on People with Disabilities,* Section 15. http://www.ncpd.org/views-news-policy/policy/church/bishops/pastoral

29. Ibid., Section 8.

30. http://www.ncpd.org/about

31. "A Celebration of That All May Enter," 2000. https://www.pcusa.org/resource/celebration-all-may-enter/

32. "Living into the Body of Christ," 2006. https://www.pcusa.org/site_media/media/uploads/_resolutions/living-into-the-body-of-christ.pdf

33. My own denominational affiliation is ELCA and I teach at an ELCA university.

34. "Social Messages." http://www.elca.org/Faith/Faith-and-Society/Social-Messages#sthash.6oBCgZ2D.dpuf

35. Ronald Duty, "Actions Taken by the ELCA and Its Predecessor Churches Regarding Persons with Disabilities and Disability Ministries," pp. 3–4.

36. *Pastoral Statement of U.S. Catholic Bishops,* Section 3.

37. "A Celebration of That All May Enter."

38. Ibid.

39. Evangelical Lutheran Church in America, "People Living with Disabilities," p. 4. http://www.elca.org/Faith/Faith-and-Society/Social-Messages/People-Living-with-Disabilities

40. Ibid., p. 14.

41. Michael Lipka, "What Surveys Say about Worship Attendance—and Why Some Stay Home," Pew Research Center, September 13, 2003. http://www.pewresearch.org/fact-tank/2013/09/13/what-surveys-say-about-worship-attendance-and-why-some-stay-home/

42. Melinda Jones Ault, Belva C. Collins, and Erik W. Carter, "Congregational Participation and Supports for Children and Adults with Disabilities: Parent Perceptions," *Intellectual and Developmental Disabilities,* 51:1, 2013, p. 50.

43. Ibid.

44. Ibid., p. 55.

Chapter Seven: Congregations and Ministry for People with Disabilities: Three Approaches

1. Thanks to Jacqueline Bussie for the recommendation.

2. Reynolds Price, *A Whole New Life.* New York: Scribner, 2003, p. 43.

3. Ibid.

4. Ibid., p. 91.

5. Thomas Reynolds, *Vulnerable Communion.* Nashville: Brazos Press, 2008, p. 41.

6. Thomas Reynolds, "Invoking Deep Access: Disability beyond Inclusion in the Church," *Dialog: A Journal of Theology,* 51:3, Fall 2012, p. 213.

7. Ibid., p. 214.

8. Erik Carter, *Including People with Disabilities in Faith Communities.* Baltimore: Brookes Publishing, 2007, p. vii.

9. "Pre-Mass: Sue Abderholden," St. Joan of Arc, May 3, 2015. http://www.saint joanofarc.org/events/pre-mass-speakers/11023/pre-mass-sue-abderholden

10. http://www.saintjoanofarc.org/pastoral-care/mental-health-ministry

11. Interview with Mary Ann Kelly-Wright, August 7, 2015.

12. http://www.bethlehem-church.org/care-ministries/mental-health-ministry

13. Interview, June 30, 2015.

14. "Bethlehem Lutheran and St. Joan of Arc Catholic Community Collaborative Mental Health Ministry," 2015 events schedule. http://www.saintjoanofarc .org/sites/default/files/file_attach/2015MHMMondayschedule.pdf

15. Interview, June 30, 2015.

16. "Pre-Mass: Sue Abderholden."

17. Ibid.

18. Ibid.

19. Reynolds, "Invoking Deep Access," p. 218.

20. "Make It OK: Make It OK: Stigma & Mental Illness," TPT, October 25, 2013. http://www.mnvideovault.org/mvvPlayer/customPlaylist2.php?id=25281&select _index=0&popup=yes#8

21. Ibid.

22. Ibid.

23. Interview, June 30, 2015.

24. "Catholic Social Teaching," U.S. Conference of Catholic Bishops, http:// www.usccb.org/beliefs-and-teachings/what-we-believe/catholic-social-teaching/; provided by Mary Ann Kelly-Wright.

25. "Major Themes from Catholic Social Teaching." http://www.cctwincities .org/MajorThemesCatholicSocialTeaching; provided by Mary Ann Kelly-Wright.

26. Interview, June 30, 2015.

27. Kansas School for the Deaf. http://www.ksdeaf.org

28. "Our Mission," Deaf Cultural Center. http://www.deafculturalcenter.org/ our-mission/

29. Marcel Broesterhuizen, "Faith in Deaf Culture," *Theological Studies*, 66, 2005, p. 312.

30. Ibid., p. 313.

31. Broesterhuizen quotes pastor Elizabeth Von Trapp Walker's reading of Exodus 4:11, for example.

32. Email, Debbie Buchholz, September 2, 2015.

33. Ibid.

34. Ibid.

35. *Americans with Disabilities: 2010.* http://www.census.gov/prod/2012pubs/p70 -131.pdf. The study suggests that Deaf or hearing-impaired adults are much less likely to be employed than hearing adults. Thus, as Buchholz argues, the ability of Deaf congregations relying largely on the contributions of Deaf members to independently financially support a church is likely to be less robust than that of congregations of hearing people, or Deaf congregations supported financially by hearing congregations.

36. Over 90 percent of Deaf children are born to hearing parents, according to the National Institute on Deafness and Other Communication Disorders; note that even in this descriptor from the Department of Health and Human Services, Deafness is regarded as a disorder. http://www.nidcd.nih.gov/health/statistics/pages/quick.aspx

37. Broesterhuizen, "Faith in Deaf Culture," p. 317.

38. Ibid.

39. "About." Deaf International Community Church, http://dicommunitychurch.org/About.html

40. Reynolds, "Invoking Deep Access," p. 221.

41. Email, Debbie Buchholz, September 2, 2015.

42. "About." Deaf International, http://www.deafinternational.org/about.html

43. Email, Debbie Buchholz, September 2, 2015.

44. Ibid.

45. See Chapter 5.

46. Broesterhuizen, "Faith in Deaf Culture," p. 307.

47. Ibid.

48. Ibid., p. 308.

49. Email, Debbie Buchholz, September 2, 2015.

50. Ibid.

51. Ibid.

52. See Chapter 5.

53. Email, Debbie Buchholz, September 2, 2015.

54. Broesterhuizen, "Faith in Deaf Culture," pp. 320–322.

55. "Staff." Deaf International Community Church, http://dicommunitychurch.org/Staff.html

56. Reynolds, "Invoking Deep Access," p. 220.

57. Broesterhuizen, "Faith in Deaf Culture," p. 323.

58. "Spirit Matters!" http://www.rejoiceomaha.org/content.cfm?id=349

59. "Spirit Matters!" handout provided by Carol Tillman.

60. Ibid.

61. Jeff Farve, "Join the Dance," *The Lutheran*, August 2003. www.thelutheran.org

62. Ibid.

63. "Things That Matter," podcast, April 17, 2013. http://thingsthatmatterland.com/things/things-that-matter-april-17-2013-carol-tillman/

64. "Spirit Matters!" http://www.rejoiceomaha.org/content.cfm?id=349

65. Ibid.

66. "Things That Matter," podcast, April 17, 2013.

67. Reynolds, "Invoking Deep Access," p. 217.

68. "Spirit Matters! Training Guide 2014–15," provided by Carol Tillman.

69. Ibid.

70. Ibid.

71. Ibid.

72. "Things That Matter."
73. Ibid.
74. Reynolds, "Invoking Deep Access," p. 221.
75. Ibid., p. 222.

Chapter Eight: Conclusions: What, Then, of God?

1. John Swinton, "Theologies of Disability: Challenges and New Possibilities," *International Journal of Practical Theology*, 14:2, January 2001.
2. Ibid., p. 277.
3. Ibid.
4. Ibid., p. 286.
5. Ibid., p. 288.
6. Ibid.
7. Ibid., p. 291.
8. Ibid., p. 295.
9. Ibid., p. 296.
10. Ibid., p. 301.
11. Ibid.
12. Ibid., p. 304.
13. Ibid., p. 306.
14. Theodore Tappert, ed. and trans., *Luther: Letters of Spiritual Counsel.* Louisville, KY: Westminster John Knox, 1955, p. 59.
15. John Swinton, *Dementia: Living in the Memories of God.* Grand Rapids: Eerdmans, 2012.

Bibliography

"A Celebration of That All May Enter," 2000, Presbyterian Church (USA). https://www.pcusa.org/resource/celebration-all-may-enter/.

"Americans with Disabilities: 2010," http://www.census.gov/prod/2012pubs/p70-131.pdf.

Annandale, Naomi, and Carter, Erik. "Disability and Theological Education: A North American Study." *Theological Education* 8(2): 83–102, 2014.

Asch, Adrienne. "Prenatal Diagnosis and Selective Abortion: A Challenge to Practice and Policy." *American Journal of Public Health* 11(89): 1649–57, 1999.

Ault, Melinda Jones, Collins, Belva C., and Carter, Erik W. "Congregational Participation and Supports for Children and Adults with Disabilities: Parent Perceptions." *Intellectual and Developmental Disabilities* 51(1): 48–61, 2013.

Ault, Melinda Jones, Collins, Belva C., and Carter, Erik W. "Factors Associated with Participation in Faith Communities for Individuals with Developmental Disabilities and Their Families." *Journal of Religion, Disability, and Health* 17(2): 184–211, 2013.

Becker, Amy Julia. "North Dakota's Abortion Ban Is a Bad Way to Stop Selective Abortion," *The Atlantic*, April 2013.

"Bethlehem Lutheran and St. Joan of Arc Catholic Community Collaborative Mental Health Ministry," 2015 events schedule. http://www.saintjoanofarc.org/sites/default/files/file_attach/2015MHMMondayschedule.pdf.

Black, Kathy. *A Healing Homiletic.* Nashville: Abingdon Press. 1996.

Block, Jennie Weiss. *Copious Hosting.* New York: Continuum. 2002.

Brock, Brian. "Theologizing Inclusion: 1 Corinthians 12 and the Politics of the Body of Christ." *Journal of Religion, Disability & Health* 15(4): 351–376, 2011.

Broesterhuizen, Marcel. "Faith in Deaf Culture." *Theological Studies* 66, 2005.

Carter, Erik. *Including People with Disabilities in Faith Communities.* Baltimore: Brookes Publishing. 2007.

"Catholic Social Teaching," United States Conference of Catholic Bishops. http://www.usccb.org/beliefs-and-teachings/what-we-believe/catholic-social-teaching/.

Clark, John Lee. *Where I Stand: On the Signing Community and My DeafBlind Experience*. Minneapolis: Handtype Press. 2014.

Cohen, Nancy L. "Christian Right Enforces GOP Senators' Vote against UN Disabilities Treaty," December 6, 2012, *The Guardian*. http://www.theguardian.com/commentisfree/2012/dec/06/christian-right-republican-senators-disabled-rights-treaty.

"Convention on the Rights of Persons with Disabilities," Article 1, United Nations. http://www.un.org/disabilities/convention/conventionfull.shtml.

Creamer, Deborah. "Made in the Image of God: Rethinking Accessible to All." Lecture delivered at Lancaster Theological Seminary, April 16, 2015. https://lancasterseminary.edu/multimedia.

Creamer, Deborah. "Theological Accessibility: The Contribution of Disability." *Disability Studies Quarterly* 26(4), Fall 2006. http://dsq-sds.org/article/view/812/987\.

Davis, Lennard. *Bending Over Backwards: Disability, Dismodernism & Other Difficult Positions*. New York: New York University Press. 2002.

Deaf International Community Church, "About." http://dicommunitychurch.org/About.html.

Diericx, Erin. "Breaking Down Boundaries." God the Healer. http://god-the-healer.com/2015/05/10/breaking-down-boundaries-physcial-psychosocial-and-spiritual/.

Diericx, Erin. "Bringing People of All Abilities Together." God the Healer. http://god-the-healer.com/2015/05/24/bringing-people-of-all-abilities-together/.

Diericx, Erin. "The Calling." God the Healer. http://god-the-healer.com/the-calling/.

Diericx, Erin. "The Calling: Erin M Diericx." God the Healer. http://god-the-healer.com/the-calling/calling-ediericx/.

Diericx, Erin. "Cerebral Palsy Is a Blessing." God the Healer. http://god-the-healer.com/2015/03/25/cerebral-palsy-is-a-blessing/.

"Disability and Theological Education," *Association of Theological Schools Policy Guidelines*, p. 13. http://www.ats.edu/uploads/about-ats/documents/policy-guideline-disability-and-theological-education.pdf.

Duty, Ronald. "Actions Taken by the ELCA and Its Predecessor Churches Regarding Persons with Disabilities and Disability Ministries." 2010.

Eiesland, Nancy. *The Disabled God: Toward a Liberatory Theology of Disability*. Nashville: Abingdon Press. 1994.

Farve, Jeff. "Join the Dance," *The Lutheran*, August 2003. www.thelutheran.org.

Fox, Dov and Griffin, Christopher L. Jr., "Disability-Selective Abortion and the Americans with Disabilities Act" (2009). *Faculty Publications*. Paper 1240.

Fry Brown, Teresa. *Weary Thrones and New Songs*. Nashville: Abingdon, 2002.

Grant, Colleen. "Reinterpreting the Healing Narratives." Nancy L. Eiesland and Don E. Saliers, eds., *Human Disability and the Service of God.* Nashville: Abingdon. 1998.

Gustavo Gutiérrez. *A Theology* of Liberation. Maryknoll, NY: Orbis Books. 1988.

Herzog, Albert. " 'We Have This Ministry': Ordained Ministers Who Are Physically Disabled." Nancy L. Eiesland and Don E. Saliers, eds., *Human Disability and the Service of God.* Nashville: Abingdon. 1998.

Hursthouse, Rosalind. "Virtue Theory and Abortion," pp. 592–606. J. Perry, M. Bratman, J. M. Fischer, eds. *Introduction to Philosophy: Classical and Contemporary Readings.* Oxford: Oxford University Press. 2007.

"Introduction to the ADA." http://www.ada.gov/ada_intro.htm.

Kansas School for the Deaf. http://www.ksdeaf.org.

Lewin, Tamar. "Ohio Bill Would Ban Abortion if Down Syndrome Is Reason," *The New York Times*, August 22, 2015. http://www.nytimes.com/2015/08/23/us/ohio-bill-would-ban-abortion-if-down-syndrome-is-reason.html?_r=0.

Lipka, Michael. "What Surveys Say about Worship Attendance—And Why Some Stay Home." Pew Research Center. September 13, 2003. http://www.pewresearch.org/fact-tank/2013/09/13/what-surveys-say-about-worship-attendance-and-why-some-stay-home/.

"Living into the Body of Christ." Presbyterian Church (USA), 2006. https://www.pcusa.org/site_media/media/uploads/_resolutions/living-into-the-body-of-christ.pdf.

Lombardo, Paul A. *Three Generations, No Imbeciles.* Baltimore, Maryland: Johns Hopkins University Press. 2010.

Luther, Martin. *Luther's Works: Table Talk Volume 54.* Philadelphia: Fortress Press. 1967.

Luther. Directed by Eric Till. Beverly Hills, CA: Metro-Goldwyn-Mayer Studios. 2003. DVD.

"Lutherans Drop Plan to Bar Disabled Clergy," *The New York Times,* September 12, 1985. http://www.nytimes.com/1985/09/12/us/lutherans-drop-plan-to-bar-disabled-clergy.html?pagewanted=print.

"Major Themes from Catholic Social Teaching." Catholic Charities of St. Paul and Minneapolis. http://www.cctwincities.org/MajorThemesCatholicSocialTeaching, provided by Mary Ann Kelly-Wright.

"Make It OK: Stigma & Mental Illness," Twin Cities PBS (TPT), October 25, 2013. http://video.tpt.org/video/23651100009/.

McBryde Johnson, Harriet. "Unspeakable Conversations," *The New York Times*, February 16, 2003.

Melcher, Sarah J. "Visualizing the Perfect Cult." Nancy L. Eiesland and Don E. Saliers, eds., *Human Disability and the Service of God.* Nashville: Abingdon. 1998.

Midelfort, H. C. Erik. "Religious Melancholy and Suicide," *Madness, Melancholy, and the Limits of the Self.* Madison: University of Wisconsin Law School. 1996.

Montopoli, Brian. "UN Treaty on Disabilities Falls Short in Senate," December 4, 2012. CBS News. www.cbsnews.com http://www.cbsnews.com/news/un-treaty-on-disabilities-falls-short-in-senate/.

National Council on Disability. "The Impact of Disability on Parenting," *Rocking the Cradle: Ensuring the Rights of Parents with Disabilities and Their Children*. 2012. https://www.ncd.gov/publications/2012/Sep272012/Ch12.

National Council on Disability. "NCD Statement on the Convention on the Rights of Persons with Disabilities (CRPD)," July 4, 2014. http://www.ncd.gov/publications/2014/07142014/.

1980 Reports and Actions of the Tenth General Convention of the American Lutheran Church.

"Our Mission." Deaf Cultural Center. http://www.deafculturalcenter.org/our-mission/.

Parens, Erik, and Asch, Adrienne. "Disability Rights Critique of Prenatal Genetic Testing: Reflections and Recommendations." *Mental Retardation and Developmental Disabilities Research Reviews* 9: 40–47, 2003.

Pastoral Statement of U.S. Catholic Bishops on People with Disabilities. National Catholic Partnership on Disability. http://www.ncpd.org/views-news-policy/policy/church/bishops/pastoral.

"People Living with Disabilities." Evangelical Lutheran Church in America, 2010. http://www.elca.org/Faith/Faith-and-Society/Social-Messages/People-Living-with-Disabilities.

Pinn, Anthony, ed. *Liberation Theologies in the United States*. New York: New York University Press, 2010.

Powell, Robyn. "Can Parents Lose Custody Simply Because They Are Disabled?" *GPSolo* 31(2), March/April 2014.

"Pre-Mass: Sue Abderholden." St. Joan of Arc Catholic Community, May 3, 2015. http://www.saintjoanofarc.org/events/pre-mass-speakers/11023/pre-mass-sue-abderholden.

Price, Reynolds. *A Whole New Life*. New York: Scribner. 2003.

Ramsey, William M. *Four Modern Prophets*. Louisville: Westminster John Knox. 1986.

Raphael, Rebecca. *Biblical Corpora: Representations of Disability in Hebrew Bible Literature*. London: Bloomsbury. 2008.

Rapp, Emily. "A New Baby Doesn't, and Shouldn't, Replace What's Lost," *The New York Times*, March 13, 2014. http://parenting.blogs.nytimes.com/2014/03/13/dragon-mother-emily-rapp-a-new-baby-doesnt-and-shouldnt-replace-whats-lost/?_r=0.

Rapp, Emily. *Poster Child*. New York: Bloomsbury, 2007.

Rapp, Emily. "Rick Santorum, Meet My Son," *Slate*, February 27, 2012. http://www.slate.com/articles/double_x/doublex/2012/02/rick_santorum_and_prenatal_testing_i_would_have_saved_my_son_from_his_suffering_.html.

"Remembering the Poor: An Interview with Gustavo Gutiérrez." *America: The National Catholic Review*. February 3, 2003. http://americamagazine.org/issue/420/article/remembering-poor-interview-gustavo-gutirrez.

Reynolds, Thomas. "Invoking Deep Access: Disability beyond Inclusion in the Church." *Dialog: A Journal of Theology* 51(3), Fall 2012.

Reynolds, Thomas. *Vulnerable Communion*. Grand Rapids: Brazos Press. 2008.

Santorum, Rich. "Problematic Disabilities Treaty up for Consideration Again," *Roll Call*, August 4, 2014. http://www.rollcall.com/news/Rick-Santorum-CRPD -and-his-daughter-Bella-235504-1.html.

"Santorum: U.N. Disabilities Treaty Would've Had Bureaucrats Unseat Parents," *The Daily Beast*, December 5, 2012. www.thedailybeast.com.

Satterlee, Craig. "About Craig." http://craigasatterlee.com/about-craig.html.

Satterlee, Craig. "Indeed, Bishop Satterlee Is Legally Blind." http://craigas atterlee.com/yes-craig-is-blind.pdf.

Satterlee, Craig. "Learning to Picture God from Those Who Cannot See." *Homiletic* 36(1), 2011.

Satterlee, Craig. " 'The Eye Made Blind': The Language of Disability in Worship." *Liturgy* 25(2), 2009.

Smeltzer, Suzanne. "Pregnancy in Women with Physical Disabilities." *Journal of Obstetrics, Gynecology, and Neonatal Nursing* 36(2), January/February 2007.

"Social Messages." Evangelical Lutheran Church in America. https://www.elca.org/ Faith/Faith-and-Society/Social-Messages.

"Spirit Matters! Training Guide 2014–15." Provided by Carol Tillman.

"Staff." Deaf International Community Church. http://dicommunitychurch.org/ Staff.html.

Steward, Raedorah. "Biographical Sketch," *UBE: Purple Yam*. http://ube-purpleyam. blogspot.com/p/biographical-sketch.html.

Steward, Raedorah. "Made by God, Broken by Life: Developing an African American Hermeneutic for Disability," *Tikkun*, November 7, 2014. http:// www.tikkun.org/nextgen/made-by-god-broken-by-life-developing-an-african -american-hermeneutic-for-disability.

Steward, Raedorah. "What Is 'the Egypt United Methodist Church?' " Delivered January 16, 2011. http://www.bloominthedesert.org/voiceswritings.html.

Swinton, John. *Dementia: Living in the Memories of God*. Grand Rapids: Eerdmans. 2012.

Swinton, John. "Theologies of Disability: Challenges and New Possibilities." *International Journal of Practical Theology* 14(2), January 2001.

Tappert, Theodore, ed. and trans. *Luther: Letters of Spiritual Counsel*. Louisville, KY: Westminster John Knox. 1955.

"Things That Matter," podcast, April 17, 2013. http://thingsthatmatterland.com/ things/things-that-matter-april-17-2013-carol-tillman/.

Tillich, Paul. "On Healing," *The New Being*. Lincoln, NE: Bison Books. 2005.

Tillich, Paul. *Systematic Theology III*. Chicago: The University of Chicago Press. 1976.

U.S. Court of Appeals for the Eighth Circuit. *MKB Management Corp., Doing Business as Red River Women's Clinic; Kathryn L. Eggleston, M.D.* http://sblog.s3 .amazonaws.com/wp-content/uploads/2015/07/ndopinion.pdf.

Walker, Robert L. *SPEAKING OUT: Gifts of Ministering Undeterred by Disabilities*. Charleston, SC: CreateSpace Independent Publishing Platform. 2012.

Watt, Jeffrey. *Choosing Death: Suicide and Calvinism in Early Modern Geneva*. Kirksville, MO: Truman State University Press, 2001.

Weber, Kerry. "Religion Update Fall 2012: In Profile," *Publishers Weekly*, August 2012.

Yong, Amos. *The Bible, Disability, and the Church*. Grand Rapids: Erdmans. 2011.

Index

About the Author

Courtney Wilder earned a PhD in systematic theology from the University of Chicago, where she was a Junior Fellow at the Martin Marty Center. She teaches in the Religion Department at Midland University in Fremont, Nebraska. She is a past president of the North American Paul Tillich Society, and is active in Lutheran theological circles. She has written on Christianity and contemporary culture, disability theology, and theologies of the body. Recent publications include "From 'Thrift Shop' to the Zero Waste Home: Popular Culture, Subversion of the Ordinary Economy, and Economy of Grace," in *The Gift of Theology: The Theological Contribution of Kathryn Tanner,* coedited by Rosemary Carbine and Hilda Koster, published in 2015; "The Courage to Be … a Dirty Little Freak: Tillich, Pink, and Gaga," in *God and Popular Culture: A Behind-the-Scenes Look at the Entertainment Industry's Most Influential Figure,* coedited by Stephen Butler Murray and Aimée Upjohn Light, published by Praeger in 2015; and "What Makes Music Christian? Hipsters, Contemporary Christian Music, and Secularization," coauthored with Jeremy Rehwaldt, in *Understanding Religion and Popular Culture,* edited by Dan Clanton Jr. and Terry Clark, published in 2012.